DEATH VALLEY
HOTTEST PLACE ON EARTH

by Roger Naylor

RIO NUEVO
PUBLISHERS

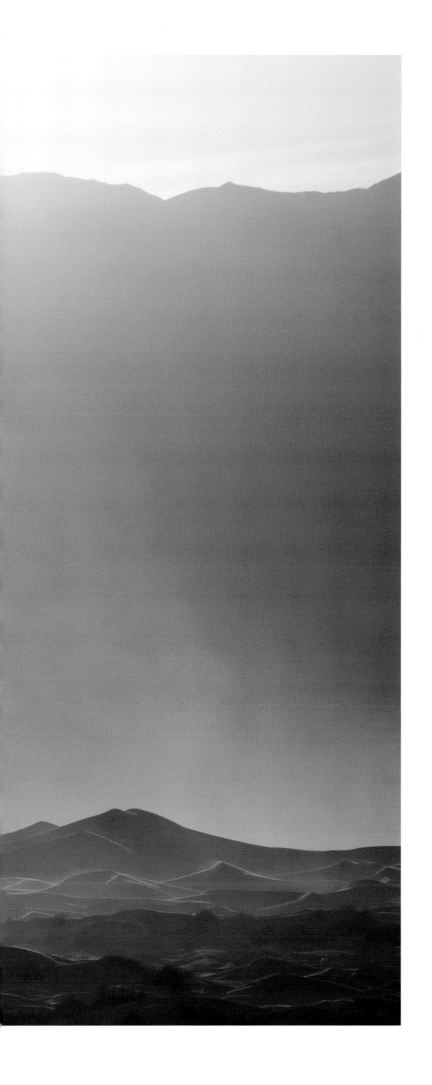

INTRODUCTION

Let's be clear: Death Valley is a stunning, beautiful place of immense diversity with an ideal climate several months of the year. And what's not to love about seventy degrees in January? Much of autumn is deliciously mild and spring can be balmy and occasionally heralded by wave after wave of colorful wildflowers. Winter even includes high mountain peaks mantled in snow. Summers, however, are a different story.

More than just a name, Death Valley is truth in advertising. This is the bad boy of deserts. Staggering extremes are the norm. Rising mountains and falling valley floors create the defining drama. The knife-blade peaks of the Panamint Mountains loom above Badwater Basin, two miles of whiplash-inducing elevation change. That's twice what occurs at the Grand Canyon.

Amid the expanse of Death Valley is an endless assortment of dramatic scenery. You'll find deep rugged canyons, haunting badlands, sand dunes, lakebeds, craters, and even flowing streams and fragile wetlands. Nearly one thousand native plant species dot the landscape and dozens of animal species prowl the hills.

A swirling, sky-blotting sandstorm adds a touch of drama to an already dramatic landscape over the dunes of Mesquite Flat.

1

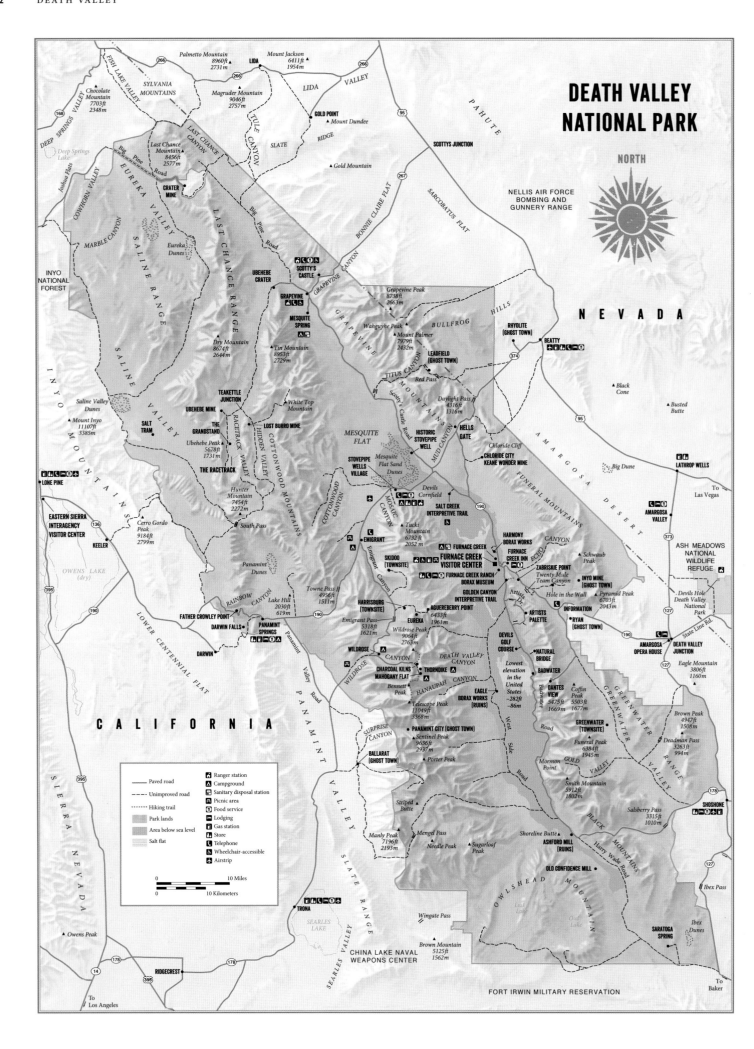

DEATH VALLEY NATIONAL PARK

NORTH

NELLIS AIR FORCE BOMBING AND GUNNERY RANGE

N E V A D A

C A L I F O R N I A

Legend:
- Paved road
- --- Unimproved road
- ···· Hiking trail
- Park lands
- Area below sea level
- Salt flat

- Ranger station
- Campground
- Sanitary disposal station
- Picnic area
- Food service
- Lodging
- Gas station
- Store
- Telephone
- Wheelchair-accessible
- Airstrip

0   10 Miles
0   10 Kilometers

FORT IRWIN MILITARY RESERVATION

FAST FACT

Most experts agree that the mysterious word "Panamint" comes from the Southern Paiute word for a division of Shoshone who lived there: "pa" meaning water, and "niwitsi" meaning person. Since they lived in the mountains, they would logically be known as the "water people."

Then summer crashes the party and it turns hot. The sun swells to the size of a manhole cover in the sky, and temperatures climb into triple digits. But it's a dry heat. Good lord, is it ever a dry heat! So dry you can stand on the salt flats and hear the ground cracking and popping around you, like the Earth smacking parched lips.

It is a thuggish, ferocious heat. It is a heat that wilts your bones and peels the enamel from your teeth. It is a heat that punches you in the stomach and steals your lunch money. Summers are long and they're hot. While the sun might be ninety-three million miles away from most of the planet, stand in the middle of Death Valley and you can hit it with a well-thrown rock.

Death Valley is the hottest place on the globe.

Ponder that for a second. Death Valley is hotter than the tropics, hotter than the Australian Outback, hotter than the Sahara Desert. A temperature of 134 degrees Fahrenheit (56 C), the highest ever, was recorded at Furnace Creek in 1913. (Keep in mind that official temperatures are recorded in the shade several feet above the ground.) During 2001, 154 consecutive days topped 100 degrees Fahrenheit. That's over five straight months of triple digits!

HOT ENOUGH FOR YOU?

"You might enjoy a trip to Death Valley, now! It has all the advantages of hell without the inconveniences."
— THE DEATH VALLEY
CHUCK-WALLA, 1907

Death Valley is a long narrow basin walled by sheer mountain ranges. With no clouds and scant vegetation to filter or soften the sunlight, it strikes with blunt force trauma and scorches a wide surface area. Heat radiates back from the rocks and soil. Warm air rises but doesn't get far. The valley's steep

walls confine the rising hot air. It cools slightly, thus sinking again where it becomes compressed by the low-elevation air pressure and undergoes additional heating.

These moving masses of superheated air, trapped by atmospheric pressure and mountains, continue to waft through the valley creating extreme high temperatures. It makes for a cruel and scorching cycle.

HOW DRY I AM

Blame the extreme dryness on simple geography. Storms form in the Pacific Ocean and roll inland. Along the way they cross a series of mountain ranges, forcing clouds to rise. As the clouds push upwards, they cool and the moisture condenses to fall as rain or snow on western slopes. By the time the clouds reach the east side of the mountains they have spent their available moisture, creating a dry "rainshadow."

Four major north-south mountain ranges create an effective cloud-spearing blockade between the ocean and Death Valley, each one adding to an increasingly drier rainshadow effect. Death Valley receives less than two inches of rain annually. Even worse, Death Valley's rate of evaporation is 150 inches per year. A twelve-foot deep lake with no other source of water would turn to a dust bowl in a year. It's a dry heat.

RECLAIMING THE TITLE

When Death Valley hit 134 degrees Fahrenheit (56.6 C) in 1913, it was the highest surface temperature ever recorded. Yet a mere eight years later, a reading of 136.4 (58 C) put the Libyan outpost of Al Aziziyah into the record books. Although many egghead types never bought it.

There were always suspicions in the scientific community surrounding the Libya numbers. Following an exhaustive investigation the skeptics were proven right. In 2012, the World Meteorological Organization (WMO) determined the Libya finding to be inaccurate. The areas of concern included an obsolete and unreliable thermometer, an inexperienced observer, and improper conditions. The Death Valley record, which was also thoroughly investigated, is acknowledged by the WMO as the Earth's hottest temperature. It took 91 years but the record is back in California.

Death Valley is the hottest place on the planet. That sizzling sound you notice? It's the wax in your ear canal being brought to a rolling boil. Place names like Devil's Cornfield evoke the staggering heat.

DEATH VALLEY FACT SHEET

Established: Death Valley National Monument was established in 1933 by President Herbert Hoover. In 1994, Bill Clinton signed the California Desert Protection Act that promoted Death Valley to a national park and increased the acreage.

Size: It's a big ol' place—twice as large as Delaware. The park covers 3.4 million acres across California with a triangle-shaped thrust into Nevada. It is America's largest national park outside Alaska.

Lowest elevation: Badwater Basin, at 282 feet (86 m) below sea level, is the lowest point in North America.

Highest elevation: The Panamint Mountains tower over the west side of the valley, most prominently Telescope Peak, which rises to 11,049 feet (3,367 m).

Highest temperature: A reading of 134 degrees Fahrenheit (56.6 C) was recorded on July 10, 1913, at Furnace Creek, making Death Valley the hottest place on Earth.

Even higher temperature: Death Valley's official temperature is recorded at a weather station five feet off the ground. But the ground gets hotter than the air. The highest ground temperature recorded was 201 degrees Fahrenheit (93.8 C) on July 15, 1972.

Rainfall: Barely. The average annual rainfall in Death Valley is 1.94 inches. In 1929 and 1953 no rain at all was recorded.

Snowfall: While the valley floor is the driest place in North America, the highest reaches of the Panamint Mountains can receive fifteen inches of precipitation. That translates into twenty feet of snow on Telescope Peak.

The ghostly reflection of the snow-clad Panamint Mountains can be seen in the shallow waters that collect on the valley floor following winter storms.

THE BEGINNING

MORE CONVENIENT THAN HELL

People visit national parks to escape the hustle and bustle of the everyday world. Then they flee the hustle and bustle of national parks and come to Death Valley for real solitude.

Nothing prepares you for the scope of the landscape. With 95 percent of Death Valley designated as wilderness, this terrain remains fierce and untamed. Sudden mountains are bracketed by the sultry curves of alluvial fans. A sea of spindly creosote washes up against slanted cliffs with swirls of strata like the grains of exotic woods. Soft gnawed badlands slouch across the valley floor, and desert winds etch intricate patterns into shifting sand dunes.

Official scenic vistas are scattered through the park but honestly, who needs

FAST FACT *The creosote bush is the predominant plant of the Mojave Desert. Their oddly formal spacing is a survival technique. To eliminate competition for scarce water each creosote bush secretes a poison (related to coal tar) that prevents new plants from taking root in its territory.*

Perhaps more than any other national park, Death Valley puts the textures of the land on display, such as the silken dunes of Mesquite Flat.

7

them? Yank the car to the shoulder, climb out, and drink in the magnificent wildness of it just about anywhere you like. Desert rolls away in all directions, stark and epic, subtle and hypnotic. It's only sun, stone, and sky, but nowhere on earth does the combination prove so devastating.

GEOLOGY CRIB NOTES

Death Valley inspires me to admit something I never thought I'd say: I wish I had stayed awake more often in science class.

A visit to the park prompts a slew of geology questions I can't answer. But then I'm not the only one to be baffled by this rocky riot. Levi Noble was a pioneering geologist who found the jumble of stone in the Black Mountains so complexly folded and faulted, he christened it "Amargosa Chaos."

Death Valley is beloved by geologists because it puts everything on display. While other national parks hide their attributes under grass, brush, and trees, Death Valley has no modesty. This is a land skinned, laid open, and bare with all the cogs and gears showing. Here are a few geology basics.

The landscape of Death Valley came about through slow, massive changes over the eons. The oldest rocks date back 1.7 billion years, relics of the Precambrian Era, and can be found in the Black Mountains. During the Paleozoic Era (300 to 500 million years ago), a warm, shallow sea covered the region leaving behind marine sediment and fossils.

Over time the sea began to recede, replaced by rising mountains and erupting volcanoes. This uplift was triggered by a collision of tectonic plates. The Earth's crust is composed of interconnected plates that are slowly pushed by currents of molten rock deep inside the planet. As the Pacific plate slid under the western edge of the North American continent, hot magma bubbled to the surface and the crumpled

crust built mountains and formed a chain of volcanoes.

Eventually the dynamics of crustal movement began to change. Plates that had been compressing began pulling apart, fracturing the crust and creating large faults. Along these north-south trending faults, mountains have uplifted and valleys down-dropped. This distinctive repetition of block-faulted valleys and mountains characterize the Basin and Range Province that reaches from Utah to California, and covers most of the western United States and northern Mexico.

Just as quickly as the mountains rise they are assailed by erosional forces trying to tear them down. Water sweeps rocks, gravel, sand, and silt from higher elevations to the valley floor. And this has been going on for millions of years. The bedrock of Badwater Basin is covered in nine thousand feet of accumulated sediments and salts. Yet the geological forces stretching the Earth's crust are still at work. The basin drops faster than it fills. The lowest point in North America is just getting lower.

During the last major Ice Age, Death Valley was filled by a series of large lakes, collectively known as Lake Manly. Waves, whipped by wind, carved terraces into Shoreline Butte still visible today. The evaporation of Lake Manly, which dried up about ten thousand years ago, left vast fields of salt deposits.

More recently, hot steam explosions blew open craters near Grapevine Canyon. Faulting and erosion continued to shape the land. Then visitors showed up.

CREOSOTE

Don't let their scraggly appearance fool you; creosote (*Larrea tridentata*) rules the Mojave Desert. As the last glacier receded from the Ice Age, the spindly ever-green was already putting down roots. The leaves are small and coated with natural oils and wax to conserve moisture. Especially pungent when wet, creosote provides the haunting perfume of a desert rain. Most impressive is the creosote's longevity. It clones itself starting from the crown, growing outward in rings. Using radiocarbon dating, one shrub in the Mojave has been assayed at 11,700 years of age.

Right: An extraordinary geologic history is etched into the hills of Zabriskie Point. **Overleaf:** The sun sets over Aguereberry Point, a high vista in the Panamints. Pete Aguereberry was a Basque miner who emigrated from France and worked the nearby Eureka Mine for 40 years.

Left: Extreme conditions couldn't diminish the lust for mineral wealth. Prospectors make camp at the south end of Death Valley in 1892. **Below:** The wild burros roaming the park are the descendents of animals turned loose by prospectors.

THE '49ERS

When gold was discovered in California in 1848, it triggered a migration that put Death Valley decisively on the map. A group of pioneers bound for the goldfields arrived in Salt Lake City too late in the year of 1849 to attempt crossing the treacherous snow-choked passes of the Sierra Nevada Mountains. It had only been a couple of years since the ill-fated Donner Party was trapped among those ragged peaks. To survive, those unfortunates resorted to cannibalism.

Rather than wait until spring, the '49ers swung southwest on the Old Spanish Trail led by Captain Jefferson Hunt. But progress was slow. Many in the party broke off from the main wagon train to follow a rumored shortcut to the west.

Almost immediately they found the way blocked by a steep-sided canyon. Most re-

turned to follow the Old Spanish Trail but more than twenty wagons forged ahead. It proved to be a grueling ordeal, requiring several weeks to cross the deserts of central Nevada. The emigrants reached Death Valley in December, breaking into small groups as they traveled.

It had been two months since they struck out on their own. Their oxen were nearly starved and the pioneers weren't much better off. From Furnace Creek, one faction, "the Jayhawkers," turned north. Upon reaching the edge of the Mesquite Flat Sand Dunes they decided they would have to walk out. They slaughtered their oxen and used the wood of their wagons to cook and jerk the meat.

The Bennett-Arcan families attempted to cross the salt flats but were too weak to continue. They dispatched two of their young men—William Lewis Manly and John Rogers—to find a route over the mountains and return with supplies. The pair walked nearly 270 miles to Mission San Fernando where they bought supplies and retraced their steps to the waiting families. The journey took twenty-six days.

As the last of the pioneers climbed across the Panamint Mountains, legend says, they looked back and exclaimed, "Goodbye, Death Valley!"

JUST A THOUGHT

The Death Valley '49ers did more than slap a catchy name on the place. They infused it with an air of defiant mystique. The '49ers have become part of the fabric of the American West, not for their navigational skills but for their toughness. We celebrate that pioneer spirit. And I think I speak for most people when I say, if you aren't forced to eat your traveling companions, it is a successful journey no matter when you reach your destination.

TIMBISHA SHOSHONE

Of course, the '49ers were not the first to discover Death Valley. Native peoples have inhabited the region off and on since the end of the last ice age. For the past thousand years or so, the Timbisha Shoshone have lived in the area. The tribe subsisted by harvesting wild plants, hunting game, and migrating with the seasons. To symbolize their strong connection to the land, they used rouge paint in their ceremonies. The word timbisha means "red rock face paint" and would later become the official name of the tribe.

The arrival of miners and ranchers disrupted the self-sufficient lifestyle of the natives. Boomtowns sprang up. Anglos moved in, occupying crucial water sources. Piñon pines and mesquite trees were cut down for wood. Years of repeated intrusions resulted in clashes between the two cultures. In 1866, Congress ratified the Treaty of Ruby Valley, which established the peace while granting the United States rights-of-way across Western Shoshone territory.

Yet, despite proclamations of peace and friendship, the Timbisha were forced to learn how to survive in a new world. They worked at whatever jobs they could find such as guides, miners, and woodcutters. Women did laundry in the mining towns. During the 1920s, many tribal members helped build Scotty's Castle and Furnace Creek Inn.

The harsh land called "Death Valley" by white settlers has been the home of the Timbisha Shoshone for 1,000 years. It provided the tribe with all they needed to survive through the centuries. To them, it is a valley of life.

When Death Valley became a national monument, the Timbisha were relocated numerous times. Finally, in 1936 a residential village was established on a forty-acre tract of land at Furnace Creek. This was a start but the wheels of justice grind slowly. The tribe did not receive federal recognition until 1983 and it wasn't until 2000 when the Timbisha Shoshone Homeland Act became law.

The bill provided for the transfer of 7,500 acres of land in California and Nevada into trust for the tribe. It allows access to traditional use resources, such as the gathering of piñon pine nuts, mesquite beans, and medicinal plants. It also gives the Timbisha Shoshone an active role along with the National Park Service in the management of some of their traditional lands.

Adapting to the changing world around them, members of the Timbisha Shoshone found jobs where they could. Many helped build Scotty's Castle in the 1920s.

CHAPTER 2

MINING

HARD METALS AND SOFT LAUNDRY

Death Valley became a destination for miners as soon as it was discovered. A member of the original Bennett-Arcan party of 1849 found a curious slice of rock, which he had made into a gunsight. The blacksmith who did the work recognized the rock as pure silver. Prospectors began searching for the Lost Gunsight Mine almost immediately. In the early years, Death Valley mining met with limited success. Lack of water and fuel plus the difficulties of transportation made only the richest mines economically viable. The most profitable gold and silver mines were discovered after 1900 when the Skidoo, Rhyolite, and Keane Wonder mines became large-scale operations. Besides gold and silver, prospectors scratched the mountains for copper, lead, zinc, tungsten, and antimony (used in alloys for car batteries and solder). Most metal mining in Death Valley ended around 1915.

BORAX

Hard metals may be more glamorous but were never found in great quantity in Death Valley. The real treasure was underfoot and

Skidoo owed its existence to a gold discovery in 1906. Like all such finds in Death Valley, the ore soon played out and within a decade Skidoo was deserted.

Above left: One of the original twenty-mule team wagons used to haul borax to the railroad sits at the Borax Harmony Works.

became best known due to a temporary transportation system.

Borax is the common name for sodium tetraborate, a naturally occurring substance produced by the repeated evaporation of seasonal lakes. Borax can resemble quartz crystals, fibrous cottonballs, or earthy white powders. The first known use of borax was by eighth century Arab gold and silversmiths for soldering (used as flux) and refining precious metals. Artisans in China used it in ceramic glazes as early as the tenth century. It's also an ingredient in cosmetics, medicines, glass, insecticides, fire retardants, and building materials.

Floodwater moved soluble borates to the floor of Death Valley where evaporation has left a mixed crust of salt, borax, and alkalis. One of the earliest Death Valley borax discoveries was made in 1881 by Aaron Winters near Furnace Creek. Winters sold his claim to William Coleman who built Harmony Borax Works on the valley floor and Amargosa Borax Works near Shoshone, where cooler summers allowed borax to be processed year round.

The problem Coleman faced was how to transport millions of pounds of borax across brutal desert. The solution became the stuff of legends. Twenty-mule teams were hitched to oversize wagons that were driven 165 grueling miles to the railroad at Mojave.

Between 1883 and 1888, borax was hauled out of the valley by teams of anywhere from sixteen to twenty mules, depending on the size of the load. The famous twenty-mule team actually consisted of eighteen mules and two horses at the rear. Each team pulled loads weighing up to thirty-six tons, including twelve hundred gallons of drinking water. The rear wheels of the wagons were seven feet high and the entire unit with mules was more than one hundred feet long.

At most, the teams could travel about seventeen miles per day. The animals responded to shouted commands and to the jerkline, a tough rope attached to the bridle of the nigh leader that ran the length of the team back to the driver. The biggest danger was in rounding a sharp curve. If all mules made the turn, the power exerted could pull

Aided by a long-running advertising campaign and radio and television program, twenty-mule teams hauling borax across unforgiving desert have become an iconic image of the Old West.

the wagon off the road or overturn it. To counteract this, a few of the mules toward the end were trained to jump over the chain and pull furiously at an opposite angle. Once the wagon had safely completed the turn, the mules jumped back over the chain.

The twenty-mule teams were a success. Not a single wagon broke down. But Harmony Borax Works closed after five years when rich borax deposits were discovered closer to the railroad. By 1890, teetering on the edge of bankruptcy, Coleman sold his properties to Francis Marion Smith, who then created the Pacific Coast Borax Company.

20 MULE TEAM BORAX

20 Mule Team Borax was possibly the world's greatest, and certainly the most unlikely, advertising campaign. A young newspaperman hired by the Pacific Coast Borax Company concocted the 20 Mule Team Borax logo. The slogan was slapped on a box of laundry detergent and sales skyrocketed. It became a household name.

Housewives sick with worry over active children and husbands too clumsy to handle a chili dog have always needed guidance. That's the essence of advertising. Now they knew where to turn. They sought out those paragons of cleanliness . . . muleskinners.

Who could possibly know more about clean laundry than men who spent weeks at a time crossing scorched, alkali-crusted lands staring through swirling dust and sand at the backsides of mules? Those guys probably sat around the campfire at night agonizing over tough stains and fresh scents.

By the way, the young journalist who came up with the 20 Mule Team Borax branding logo was named Stephen Mather. He later went on to become the first director of the National Park Service.

DEATH VALLEY DAYS

It was Pacific Coast Borax Company that introduced future generations to Death Valley when they sponsored the long running syndicated western, Death Valley Days. The program was first broadcast on radio in 1930. It moved to television in 1952, where it ran through 1975.

Each episode featured "true" stories of the Wild West. If you watched westerns of that era, you know they played fast and loose with reality, shuffling legends and facts as easily as Doc Holliday handled a deck of cards.

Episodes were introduced by a host. For the first dozen years, the "Old Ranger," played by Stanley Andrews, held that job. When he left, Ronald Reagan stepped in and also appeared in acting roles on several programs. It was his final acting gig before entering politics.

Robert Taylor, Dale Robertson, and Merle Haggard all served stints as the show's host. Death Valley Days was sponsored by Pacific Coast Borax Company until it became the U.S. Borax and Chemical Corporation following a merger. Products that were touted on the show included 20 Mule Team Borax, a laundry additive; Borateem, a laundry detergent; and Boraxo, a powdered hand soap. And just like that, little bits of Death Valley landed in cupboards in households all across America.

CHAPTER 3

ATTRACTIONS A TO Z

WISH YOU WERE HERE

Despite the foreboding name, Death Valley is a remarkably accessible national park. So much scenery and so many of the primary features can be enjoyed from main roads that thread through the expanse. You can sample a great deal from the comfort of your car. From Artist's Drive to Zabriskie Point, here are some of the very best easy-to-reach attractions Death Valley offers.

ARTIST'S DRIVE

This twisting loop moseys through colorful foothills of the Black Mountains. The road clambers up an alluvial fan. Rain may be scarce here but it creates a sensation when it does arrive.

Precipitation hits the higher elevations and gets funneled into canyons that drain the mountains. The surging water gains speed, roaring through narrow channels and gathering loose material along the way. As it rushes out the canyon mouth and into the open valley, the water loses energy; it begins to drop its sediment load and spreads into multiple small streams. That apron of rocky debris at the base of the mountains is an alluvial fan. As Artist's Drive dips in and out of rain-scoured gorges, it

The lavish colors of Artist's Palette are found along Artist's Drive.

JUST A THOUGHT

Technically, Death Valley is no valley at all. A valley is carved by water. Death Valley is a graben, created by tectonic forces. Fortunately, there were no geologists among the departing 49ers so they didn't say "Goodbye, Death Graben," which lacks a certain poetry.

Left: The salt flats of Badwater basin lap against rocky slopes of the Black Mountains. The expanse of salt is the result of Lake Manly drying up after the Ice Age. **Above:** Early morning sun paints the peaks of the Panamint Mountains with a delicate light, as seen from Dante's View. **Right:** At 282 feet below sea level, Badwater basin contains the lowest spot in North America.

toon at the base of the Black Mountains, it's not actually poisonous, just salty as seawater. At 282 feet below sea level, you're standing at the lowest spot in North America. To snap things into perspective, glance up at rocky cliffs high above and you'll spot a barely legible sign that reads "Sea Level."

Stay on the boardwalk around the pool to avoid crushing the tiny snails that call this beachfront property home. Then continue on to the blinding whiteness of the flats. The saltpan—it's about ninety-five percent pure table salt—covers two hundred square miles, a scorched, crustscape of shimmering sun haze. Walk beyond crowds to gain a sense of the sprawling dimensions and utter desolation. Don't go far if it's summer, lest the heat overpower you.

DANTE'S VIEW

Anyone who grew up watching cartoons knows some sights are so remarkable they can cause your eyeballs to actually pop out of your head. From this lofty perch of Dante's View, prepare to fish for your peepers because it is a soul-squeezing panorama.

The viewpoint sits in the Black Mountains at 5,475 feet, directly above Badwater and almost due east of Telescope Peak. If possible, visit during the early morning to put the sun at your back. Photographers love catching the dawn here as that early light splashes the tops of the Panamint Range.

An unmarked but obvious trail angles north from the parking lot, climbing to the top of Dante's Peak, gaining 300 feet of elevation in a half-mile. Views from here

provides an interesting look at the inner layers of this particular fan.

The one-way loop is paved for its entire nine miles. Make the quick turn-off to Artist's Palette, a beautiful overlook of an intense spectrum of colors splashed across the furrowed hills. The reds, pinks, oranges, yellows, and browns are due to the presence of hematite, a red iron oxide, and limonite, a yellow iron oxide. The green is from chlorite, and the blue is from manganese. This is a great drive to make in the late afternoon as the colors intensify.

BADWATER

Without a stop at Badwater, you haven't really visited Death Valley at all. This is the salt-dipped heart of the park. Named for a shallow briny pool tucked like Satan's spit-

are even more spectacular. Another trail follows a ridgeline south passing outcrops of boulders that shelter sitting areas where you can pause and admire the view. Because of the elevation difference, Dante's View is usually twenty-five degrees cooler than the valley floor.

DEVIL'S CORNFIELD

Death Valley will never be mistaken for the corn belt of Iowa and driving through the Devil's Cornfield won't alter that perception. The sprawling field spreads out on both sides of the road with "corn shocks" ambling off toward distant mountains. The clumps of brush are actually arrowweed, once used by Native American tribes to make arrow shafts. Wind scours away the soil and sand at the base of the plant, creating the stack-like appearance.

Arrowweed thrives where the groundwater has a salty tinge, with roots sunk into the underground briny soup of Salt Creek. Use the designated pullouts to snap a photo or do a little exploring.

DEVIL'S GOLF COURSE

The Devil's Golf Course was once covered by an ancient saline lake. The water dried up leaving behind layers of salt that have been twisted and gnarled by the forces of erosion. Serrated spires rise in a chaotic jumble. The valley floor is a ragged, scabby terrain that seems to stretch for miles.

There are no hiking trails across the playa but you can proceed with caution. Don't damage the crystals and don't injure yourself on the sharp edges. This is not a place for flip-flops.

Death Valley swallows noise and this is one of those places where it becomes distinctly noticeable. You can see the road and its flow of traffic, but the sound of cars dies on the creosote flats. Despite the playful name, the Devil's Golf Course is a haunting spot.

A park service sign gives a bit of an

explanation for the eerie terrain and then states this disturbing fact: "Listen carefully. On a warm day you may hear a metallic cracking sound as the salt pinnacles expand and contract."

Great. Imagine you're all by yourself in this foreboding place. You wander a few tentative steps out into the jagged maze. The stillness threatens to overwhelm you. All of a sudden you hear—right behind you!—what sounds like a gun being cocked.

FATHER CROWLEY POINT

Perched on the western edge of the national park atop the Argus Mountains, this viewpoint dishes up a panorama of a vast, lonely landscape. Panamint Valley, the Panamint Mountains, and the colorful slash of Rainbow Canyon are all visible. A rough dirt track stretches from the parking lot to the

Above: A ferocious sky haunts the Devil's Cornfield. **Right:** Ragged, jagged salt spires add a dangerous, otherworldly feel to the Devil's Golf Course.

rim of the plateau and provides an elaborate geologic overview. Dark lava flows, steep-tilted mountains, and the beige blush of the Panamint Sand Dunes trapped at the north end of the valley can be seen. The point is named for Father John J. Crowley known as the "Desert Padre," who ministered in the area during the 1920s and 30s.

HARMONY BORAX WORKS

Rusting machinery, crumbling adobe walls, and the weathered hulks of big wagons sit on the shore of the salt flats near Furnace Creek. Harmony Borax Works operated from 1883 to 1888.

A loop trail circles the remains of the plant with interpretive signs explaining the work that went on. Chinese laborers gathered the borax clusters and then brought them to the plant where they were boiled in large vats as part of the refining process. The finished product was loaded into the twenty-mule team wagons and hauled 165 miles across unforgiving terrain to the railroad. The wagons out in front of the plant are the genuine article, preserved by the dry climate. It's a remarkable piece of history.

Leaving the Borax Works, turn left on a short (0.4 miles), one-way dirt road that cuts through Mustard Canyon. The rich-yellow rocks are clay deposits of the Furnace Creek Formation, veined by trace amounts of borate minerals.

MESQUITE FLAT SAND DUNES

If you watch enough western movies, you would think the desert is blanketed with sand dunes. No matter what direction the posse takes when they go after the stage coach robbers, you can bet they'll be slogging through deep sand by lunchtime.

In reality, less than 2 percent of North American deserts are covered with dunes. They're tricky things and require a few essential ingredients to exist. Not surprisingly you need an abundant supply of loose sand to start. Also required are strong winds to move the sand and a place for the sand to collect.

Death Valley has the whole dune assembly kit. Steep mountains flanking broad basins act as a barrier. They slow the momentum of sand-laden winds, forcing them to drop their gritty loads.

The Harmony Borax Works and its massive twenty-mule team wagons hauling "white gold" across the desert helped make Death Valley famous. **Right:** Smoothed by night winds and bathed in early morning light, the dunes of Mesquite Flat prove almost irresistible to Death Valley visitors.

The best known dune fields in the park, and most accessible, are the Mesquite Flat Dunes about two miles east of Stovepipe Wells. You spot them just off the road, like caramel-colored ocean waves. While the sands shift with every windstorm, the dunes are trapped in place.

Three types of dunes—crescent, linear, and star-shaped—spread across fourteen-square miles. It's a deceptive expanse that doesn't appear so large until you notice a few specks inching across the crest of the dunes and realize they're people. Park in the lot and wander out into the sand. Clumps of mesquite trees huddle in shallow gullies providing stable habitats for wildlife. Look for tracks of lizards, birds, kangaroo rats, foxes, coyotes, and the wavy parallel lines that indicate a sidewinder rattlesnake scooted across the sand. You'll catch the most intriguing light in the early morning or evening. And if you happen to be at the park during a full moon, it's well worth traipsing out here. Other dune fields are located in the Panamint Valley, Saline Valley, near the Ibex Hills, and in remote Eureka Valley.

SALT CREEK INTERPRETIVE TRAIL

This is another little corner of Death Valley that takes you by surprise. Salt Creek forms a shrubby, half-hearted oasis amid otherwise desolate badlands. For much of the year Salt Creek is nothing more than a few puddles. Yet even such a haphazard waterway manages to sustain a population of pupfish found nowhere else in the world.

A raised boardwalk curves through the marshy meadow created by Salt Creek, providing access to this shaggy oasis on the valley floor. **Above:** Fed by a series of springs, the lazy meander of Salt Creek only flows above ground for two miles but still supports a population of pupfish. **Left:** The sand dunes at Mesquite Flat cover an area nearly 15 square miles near Stovepipe Wells and are easily accessible from the highway.

Salt Creek Pupfish (*Cyprinodon salinus*) are Ice Age relics, the ecosystem crumbs left over from that era of abundance when Lake Manly covered Death Valley. As waters receded, the pupfish were left stranded in isolated pools of varying sizes, temperatures, and salt content. They managed to survive, and Death Valley now supports five species. The pupfish earned its name because of its frisky, puppy-like behavior.

A half-mile of wooden boardwalk loops through the pickleweed and salt grass surrounding the creek. This is easy walking with lots of good viewpoints. Pupfish are small—only an inch or two—and are best seen in the spring during mating season. That's when the males turn bright blue and aggressively defend their territory. And who can blame them? Nobody knows better that water is a fleeting commodity in this parched landscape.

TWENTY MULE TEAM CANYON

When it comes to short scenic roadways in Death Valley, Artist's Drive receives most of the accolades. And the traffic. That's good news for visitors savvy enough to seek out this drive because it gives them a chance to savor the undulating hills and vivid colors minus the crowds.

The road through Twenty Mule Team Canyon plunges you right into the belly of the badlands, the same ones seen from nearby Zabriskie Point. The unpaved 2.7-mile one-way route meanders through multihued buttes creased by clay-lined gullies. It is an exotic moonscape of mudstone cliffs and crumbling ridgelines. The formations push against the road in places, their graveled slopes practically leaning into the car window. Vegetation is almost nonexistent due to the alkaline nature of the soil and ongoing erosion that makes it difficult for roots to take hold.

These are some of the most distinctive badlands in the park. Hills of black, dark brown, yellow, cream, and white are spread throughout the canyon. Old prospectors' tunnels gouged into the hills have since been sealed. This was part of the Monte Blanco mining district. Despite the name of the canyon, it was not on the route taken by the famed twenty-mule teams. The Monte Blanco office that once nestled among these

Above Left: During the spring mating season, the Salt Creek pupfish are active and easier for visitors to see. **Above:** The chuckwalla is a large, plump lizard draped in baggy folds of skin. When threatened, the chuckwalla scurries into a crevice and then gulps air to inflate, thus wedging itself in. **Left:** The road through Twenty Mule Team Canyon is a twisting, curving drive that dishes up beautiful views of colorful rock layers and badlands.

Above: Formed by a violent steam explosion, colorful Ubehebe Crater is the largest of the maar volcanoes gouged from the foothills of the Cottonwood Mountains.

hills was moved to Furnace Creek where it now houses the Borax Museum.

The dirt road is easily managed by sedans but turns into a muddy mess following a rain. Of course, rainstorms are infrequent, to say the least.

UBEHEBE CRATER

Death Valley was forged eons ago. The forces of nature that tilted, twisted, and scoured this land stretch back hundreds of millions of years. The place feels ancient.

Then there are the young guns—Ubehebe Crater, Little Hebe Crater, and the rest of their volatile ilk. Clusters of volcanic craters pockmark the north end of the park at the edge of the Cottonwood Mountains. The age of the craters ranges from a few thousand years to as little as eight hundred years old, making them the new kids on the geological block.

Known as maar volcanoes, the craters were created when magma rising from the depths collided with groundwater. The intense heat flashed the water into steam, which expanded until the pressure was released as an earth-shaking explosion. Ubehebe is the largest; a gaping wound six hundred feet deep and half a mile across. The blast showered shattered rock over a six-square-mile area, burying some places to a depth of 150 feet.

A 1.5-mile trail crunches through the cinders and circles the rim of Ubehebe. From the high southern edge of the crater, a spur trail branches off to Little Hebe, perched on the backside of Ubehebe. There are also several trails that angle down from the rim into the bottom of the crater. While it's an easy walk down you'll be huffing and puffing on the way out, partly due to the climb and partly because of the shifty, slidey nature of the volcanic cinders. It's a little like trying to walk uphill across a McDonald's playland ball pit. One other word of warning: hang on to your hat. Howling winds are a common occurrence here.

The benefits of Swiss engineering can be seen in the charcoal kilns tucked away in Wildrose Canyon. Built in 1877, the ten beehive-shaped kilns are strikingly uniform in size and shape and still in excellent condition.

WILDROSE CHARCOAL KILNS

While much of Death Valley's mining past lies in various states of decay and disintegration, the charcoal kilns that line the upper end of Wildrose Canyon remain distinctly pristine. The ten beehive-shaped stone kilns were built in 1877. They supplied charcoal for two lead-silver smelters located in the Argus Range twenty-five miles away where fuel was scarce.

The kilns stand about twenty-five feet high and are thirty feet in diameter all in a tidy row. They're big dollops of stone that seem more futuristic than historic, more extraterrestrial than western . . . like Easter Island mailboxes.

Workers would fill the kilns (designed by Swiss engineers) with piñon pine logs cut from the surrounding hillsides and fire them. After a week of smoldering, about two thousand bushels of charcoal were ready to be hauled to the smelters. The kilns were only used for a couple of years, which may help account for their superb condition. Inside, the kilns still smell of smoke and the walls are blackened with soot. Also, they have great acoustics. As you walk toward the middle of the space a shimmering thrum reverberates through the structure from footsteps and voice.

SIDEWINDER

The venomous sidewinder (*Crotalus cerastes*) is best known for its sideways form of locomotion, which leaves parallel, J-shaped tracks in the sand. The hook of the "J" points in the direction of the snake's travel. They prefer sand dunes, sandy washes, or desert flats where rodents tend to burrow. Light in color with rough scales that aid them in their movement, they also have triangular projections pointed and upturned over each eye, prompting the nickname Horned Rattlesnake. But when you're known as the sidewinder, isn't a cool nickname redundant?

ZABRISKIE POINT

This is the quasi-official sunrise and sunset viewing spot for Death Valley. A short trail from the parking lot climbs to a comfortable perch where visitors savor a maze of wildly eroded badlands. Long fingers of mudstone ridges grasp at the valley floor and gather shadows in the slanted light of dawn and dusk. Perhaps more than any other spot in the park, Zabriskie Point puts the textures of the environment on display. All the depth and details of the ripples and wrinkles emerge in the softening light of sunrise and sunset, and crowds gather for both dramatic shows.

Named for Christian Zabriskie, the general manager of the Pacific Coast Borax Works, the overlook offers a stunning panorama of a barren, though striking, landscape. Bare furrowed hills spread across the desert floor. Rising above the badlands is the jutting shark tooth of a hill known as Manly Beacon. Be sure to visit for a sunset. That light, so hard and brittle at noon, melts like warm honey down the slopes of these crumpled hills as day dissolves into dusk.

Above: The rippled mudhills of Zabriskie Point spread across the desert floor. Their colors seem to evolve in changing light, making this an extremely popular spot for sunrise and sunset watchers.
Overleaf: There are many deserts. There is only one Death Valley. Epic views are visible from Aguereberry Point.

CHAPTER 4

SCOTTY'S CASTLE

A SHACK FIT FOR
A KING OF THE CON MEN

The official name is Death Valley Ranch but nobody, not even the National Park Service, calls it anything but Scotty's Castle. The lavish Spanish hacienda rises in Grapevine Canyon on the northern rim of the park. It would be impressive no matter what the setting, but nestled in this far-flung place, shaded by palm trees, it seems downright impossible, a thirty-two-thousand-square-foot mirage.

Encompassed within the castle complex is a twenty-five-room mansion that includes turrets, arched doorways, indoor fountains, and a pipe organ. Among the nine surrounding outbuildings are guesthouses, stables, and a fifty-six-foot-tall "chime tower." Despite the name, the lavish joint was never owned by anyone named Scotty. But of course, that's not the way Scotty told it.

Under normal circumstances, when a flimflam man is caught mid-swindle, he's dragged off to the hoosegow. But since this is Death Valley, normal doesn't enter into the equation. Instead of the calaboose, Walter Scott, a paunchy, yarn-spinning, dream-weaving huckster, landed in a castle.

Of all the unexpected wonders of Death Valley, nothing is more surprising than finding an elaborate Spanish Provincial style castle tucked away in Grapevine Canyon.

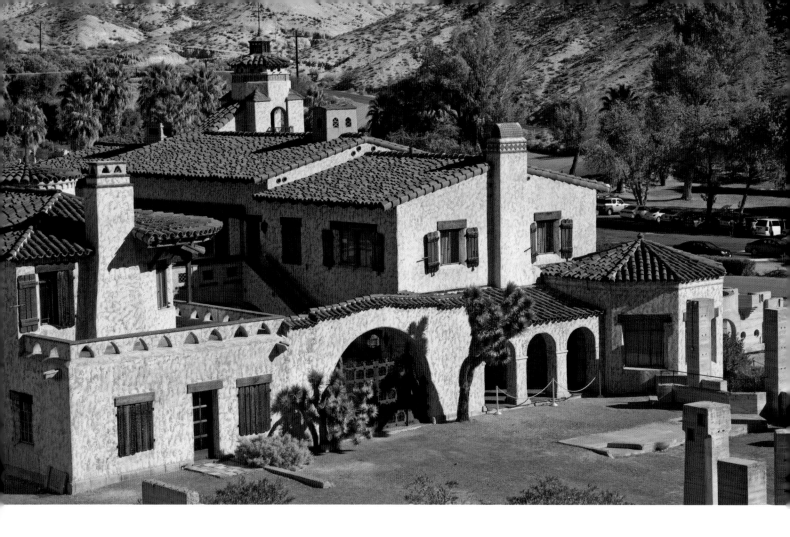

DEATH VALLEY SCOTTY

The man who would become known as Death Valley Scotty was born in Kentucky in 1872. He left home at the age of eleven, heading west to join his older brothers as a cowhand. He later worked in Death Valley as a swamper (driver's assistant) on the twenty-mule team wagons. In 1890, he signed on with the Buffalo Bill Wild West Show. For ten years Scott toured America and Europe as a trick rider with the troupe, where he learned the power of giving the audience what it wanted.

After a falling out with Buffalo Bill, Scott quit the show. But his career as an entertainer was just getting started. Using two souvenir nuggets from a Colorado gold mine, Scott conned a New York banker into giving him a grubstake. More traditional prospectors might have used the money to seek or develop mines, but Scott took an all-expense-paid vacation. He spent time exploring Death Valley but he never filed a claim nor bought any mining equipment.

Above: Construction of the castle began in 1922. Materials, equipment, and laborers all had to be transported to the far-flung location by railroad. **Left:** Despite never producing a single claim, Death Valley Scotty may have been the most famous prospector of his era.

FAST FACT

Albert Johnson originally approached famed architect Frank Lloyd Wright about designing the castle. Wright was interested and drew up some plans but they were not ornate enough for Johnson.

Above: Unlikely friendships are often the most rewarding. The loveable rascal Death Valley Scotty poses with his dear friends, the devoutly religious millionaire couple, Bessie and Albert Johnson.
Right: Tired of sleeping in tents, it was Bessie Johnson who encouraged her husband Albert to build a comfortable vacation home.

He soon rolled into Los Angeles flashing fat wads of cash, courtesy of his unsuspecting backer. Scott checked into the finest suites and rained money. He spent lavishly and tipped extravagantly, throwing C-notes around like they were nickels. Plenty more where that came from, he explained, telling everyone about his secret gold mine in Death Valley. The newspapers ate it up and the legend of Death Valley Scotty was born.

In 1905, using funds supplied by a mining promoter, Scotty chartered a special Santa Fe train to break the speed record between Los Angeles and Chicago, garnering more national attention. They completed the journey in forty-four hours and fifty-four minutes, shattering the previous record by eight hours.

"We got there so fast," said the always-quotable Scotty, "nobody had time to sober up."

THE MILLIONAIRE

Around this time one of Scotty's most loyal investors decided to see this Death Valley gold mine for himself. Albert Johnson, Chicago insurance magnate, journeyed west and was given the kind of tour of Death Valley only Scotty could give.

They were ambushed by bandits—an ambush Scotty arranged. It was an attempt to scare Johnson off. However, when the lead started flying, Scotty's brother Warner was hit. Scotty yelled for the "bushwhackers" to stop firing and they slunk away. The jig was up. Johnson now knew there was no mine. But here's where the story takes a lovely turn: he didn't care.

Blame it on the bewitching quality of Death Valley. Johnson was having the time of his life riding through untamed lands, sleeping under the stars and listening to Scotty's tales around the campfire. Johnson, who had suffered a broken back during a railroad accident, felt his health restored by the hot, dry climate. The two men became lifelong friends.

Johnson began bringing his wife, Bessie, to the region, and it was she who urged him to build more comfortable accommodations than the big tents they were using. Construction began in 1922, a massive undertaking as materials and manpower proved challenging to come by in such a remote location.

Ever the self-promoter, Scotty seized the opportunity. He told everyone that he was building a two-million-dollar castle with profits from his gold mine. Johnson, who had no yearning for the spotlight, played along and passed himself off as Scotty's banker.

The sprawling hacienda became a gracious getaway for the Johnsons. Scotty had a bedroom at the castle but preferred staying in a simple wooden cabin Johnson had built for him five miles away called Lower Vine Ranch. But whenever the Johnsons entertained you can be sure Scotty was there, regaling the guests with his adventures and extending the hospitality of his castle.

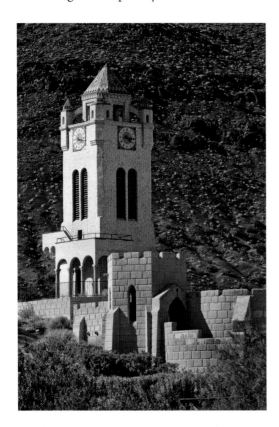

Investing in the old scoundrel's schemes turned out to be a shrewd move for the financier. As Johnson so elegantly put it, "Scotty repays me in laughs."

During the Great Depression, the castle became a popular hotel and tourist attraction as people began to explore the new Death Valley National Monument. Bessie Johnson died in 1943 and Albert passed away five years later. Having no heirs,

Left: The chimes tower features a Howard clock and a set of twenty-five chimes that can be programmed to play automatically. **Top:** Visitors can only enter Scotty's Castle during regular tours. These are conducted daily by knowledgeable rangers dressed in period clothing. **Above:** There can be no doubt that this really is Scotty's Castle. Death Valley Scotty is buried on a hill overlooking the property. Nice to know he's still keeping an eye on things.

Johnson left his entire estate to the Gospel Foundation of California, an organization the deeply religious millionaire created for the purpose. The foundation administered the affairs of the castle and continued to operate the hotel and conduct tours. They also cared for Scotty for the rest of his days, just as Johnson intended.

One of the thrills for any visitor during that era was meeting Death Valley Scotty, always the gregarious host until he died in 1954 at the age of eighty-two. He was laid to rest on a hill above the grounds. A short trail leads up to Scotty's grave, where

Right: You can't have a castle without towers. And there's no point in having a tower without a spiral staircase.
Below: If you think the exterior of Scotty's Castle is elaborate, wait until you see the inside. It is a palatial home, and the furnishings are original, making the experience even more impressive.

there is a bronze marker inscribed with his words: "I got four things to live by: Don't say nothing that will hurt anybody. Don't give advice—nobody will take it anyway. Don't complain. Don't explain."

In 1970 the National Park Service purchased Scotty's Castle, along with the rest of Albert Johnson's Death Valley property, from the Gospel Foundation.

TOURS

Scotty's Castle is open year-round. There's a visitor center, gift and snack shop, and picnic area. Admission to the grounds is free but fees are charged for tours. Park rangers dressed in period costumes conduct detail-rich informative tours. The castle is decorated with Spanish and Italian antiques, leather furniture, hand-carved redwood beams, and iron chandeliers. Custom crafted tile floors are covered with handmade Spanish Majorcan rugs. All furnishings are original. During winter and spring, hiking tours are conducted to Lower Vine Ranch.

GHOST TOWNS

LANDSCAPE SKELETONS

Decades of mining activity left scars upon Death Valley in the form of ghost towns. These crumbling wisps linger in the desert or cling to mountainsides with a rickety grip. Every piece of rusting machinery and weathered wood connects us to an era gone but not distant. Spend time poking into the past but please do not remove or disturb any of the remains.

BALLARAT

Sitting on the western edge of the national park in the Panamint Valley, Ballarat is a picturesque ghost town that still hangs on. Founded in 1897, it served as supply point and recreation center for several nearby

Left: Despite being abandoned a century ago, the rubble and ruins of Rhyolite still hang on. Nevada's most famous ghost town sits just four miles west of Beatty. **Above:** Along with crumbling foundations and weathered shacks, Ballarat is one of the few Death Valley ghost towns that still boasts a resident or two. A small store is open most afternoons and on weekends.

gold and silver mines. Named after an Australian gold camp, Ballarat was once home to four hundred people, including some of Death Valley's most colorful characters, like Shorty Harris and Seldom Seen Slim.

After the Radcliffe Mine, the biggest producer in the area, suspended operation in 1905, Ballarat began to decline. The post office closed in 1917. Still, a few of the old-timers stayed on. The cemetery contains a few unmarked graves but there's also one adorned with an elegant marker. It reads:

CHARLES FERGE
Prospector
"Seldom Seen Slim"
1889–1968
"Me lonely? Hell, no!
I'm half coyote and half wild burro!"

Although Ballarat is privately owned, visitors are still welcomed. Even today the town boasts a resident or two and a small store that's open on weekends and afternoons. Old miner cabins, some adobe ruins, and crumbling foundations still refuse to knuckle under to the elements.

Ballarat is located off the Panamint Valley Road west of Death Valley.

SHORTY HARRIS

A little guy with a big heart, Frank "Shorty" Harris was a legendary Death Valley figure, the last of the single-blanket jackass prospectors. Harris said he could smell gold. He made several notable discoveries, including his namesake Harrisburg and the area's richest strike in the Bullfrog Hills.

What he lacked was an interest in developing mines. Harris also had a nose for whiskey and was quick to sell his latest find and go on a bender, buying drinks and meals for everyone when he was in the chips. He sold his half of the Bullfrog claim for a pittance while under the influence. While Harris may not have been a shrewd businessman, he was by all accounts happy and certainly had a wealth of friends. When he died in 1934 at the age of seventy-four, hundreds attended his funeral. He was buried, per his request, on the floor of Death Valley alongside his old pal Jim Dayton. Shorty Harris once summed up his philosophy like this: "Who the hell wants ten million dollars? It's the game, man—the game." Viva la Shorty!

Despite their vilification in horror movies, tarantulas are shy creatures. A tarantula bite is generally no more serious than a bee sting.

Left: Allegedly, this weathered truck in Ballarat belonged to Charlie Manson, or at least to one of his followers. The Manson Family was camping at the nearby Barker Ranch when they were arrested. **Bottom:** The old smelter chimney forms a distinctive exclamation point among the ruins of Panamint City.

SKIDOO

The greatest name for a ghost town. Ever.

Skidoo was founded in 1906 when two prospectors were on their way to the gold strike in Harrisburg. While camping near Emigrant Spring they discovered rock ledges freckled with gold. As the town sprang up, more water was needed for milling and mining than what Emigrant Spring could provide. A plan was devised for a pipeline to be built bringing water from the Panamint Mountains, some twenty-three miles away. Thus, "23 Skidoo," an American slang term meaning to "get out fast."

Skidoo proved to be a bustling town for several years reaching a population of seven hundred. Among the many businesses were saloons, a sawbones, grocery and hardware stores, and even a newspaper. (*Skidoo Times*? *Daily Skidoo*?) By 1917, the rich vein played out and the mine closed for good.

Despite the playful moniker, Skidoo was the site of Death Valley's only two hangings. Even stranger, both times it was the same guy getting his neck stretched.

Hootch Simpson—and wouldn't you know a town called Skidoo would hang a guy named Hootch?—was a saloon owner who hit a rough patch. He tried to rob the bank, failed, and killed a store owner. During the night the townsfolk (Skidooans? Skidooites? Skidoobies?) hanged him. And then hanged him again. So goes the legend. The second necktie party was to accommodate news reporters who missed the first one.

PANAMINT CITY

It was called the "toughest, rawest, most hard-boiled little hell-hole that ever passed for a civilized town."

Outlaws hiding out in Surprise Canyon discovered silver in 1873 and parlayed that

into an amnesty deal, after agreeing to pay back their stolen money from mining profits. By 1874 Panamint City was booming, with two thousand people strung along a muddy, rutted, mile-long main street.

No surprise that the town developed a wild and wooly reputation with bandits for founding fathers. Reportedly, fifty shootings took place during Panamint City's short life. Wells Fargo refused to open an office. To ship the ore without it being stolen, silver bullion was cast in cannon-like balls that weighed in excess of four hundred pounds. Not the kind of thing that can be carried off by a man on horseback.

By 1876 much of the ore had been depleted. And in July of that year a heavy storm sent a wall of water roaring through the canyon destroying most of the town. That marked the end of Panamint City, although the mines were worked off and on for years.

The most prominent remains from that era are the towering chimney of the smelter and some crumbling walls. There's also rusted equipment and structures from more recent mining activity. Today the ruins of Panamint City are only accessible via an arduous five-mile hike from Chris Wicht's Camp, which is located six miles northeast of Ballarat.

Above: In 1907, residents and ball players of Skidoo move a piano in preparation for a lively July 4th celebration. **Left:** While virtually nothing remains from the townsite of Skidoo, the skeleton of the massive stamp mill still clings to a nearby hillside.

LEADFIELD

You can't have a boom without a bust. And no Death Valley boomtown busted faster than Leadfield. A few mining claims were filed in 1905 but were soon abandoned due to the remoteness of the location. It wasn't until 1926 when serious mining began. Western Lead Mines hit a promising ledge of ore. Stock shares were sold as speculation heated up.

Some three hundred hopeful souls made their way to this rocky gash in the Grapevine Mountains. Flamboyant oil promoter C. C. Julian became the president of Western Lead and his marketing prowess brought plenty of attention to Leadfield. He printed up handbills of ships piled high with ore steaming down the Amargosa River. (In reality, the Amargosa flows mostly underground.) He brought in trainloads of potential investors. The post office opened in August of 1926. The future looked bright. Four months later the post office closed and the town was virtually empty.

Julian's financial fortunes tanked due to some shady stock dealings, just about the time the ore played out in the main mines. As quickly as folks showed up, they vanished. Because of how things developed, C. C. Julian has been called a flimflam man by some, a scapegoat by others. But the big legacy of that abrupt boom-bust era is the Titus Canyon Road that would never have been built without the lure of big wealth, whether real or imagined. Today, it's one of the favorite drives for Death Valley visitors.

Leadfield sits below Red Pass, a few wood and tin shacks clinging to a hillside, along with dugouts, foundations, and mine dumps. From the parking area a series of pathways weave among the peaceful ruins of this tumbledown town.

RHYOLITE

In 1904, Shorty Harris and Ed Cross were prospecting in the area and found quartz. As Shorty described it, "the quartz was just full of free gold . . . it was the original bullfrog rock . . . this banner is a crackerjack." The Bullfrog Mining District was established and the rush was on.

The fast-growing town of Rhyolite was named for the silica-rich volcanic rock so prominent in the area. Called the "Queen City of Death Valley," the town once overflowed with eight thousand residents who enjoyed a wide-ranging social scene from baseball games to symphonies to whist parties to a red light district that drew women from as far away as San Francisco. The financial panic of 1907 sent shock waves through Rhyolite. The mines began closing and the town was virtually deserted a few years later. Today numerous ruins remain, including the lanky three-story skeleton of the bank building and Tom Kelly's famed bottle house.

Above: Titus Canyon Road brushes past the scattered debris of Leadfield. **Bottom:** A few wobbly shacks and cabins clinging to the hillsides are all that remains of Leadfield, one of Death Valley's more meteoric boomtowns. **Right:** The haughty shambles of the former bank building anchors the once booming city of Rhyolite.

In 1906, Kelly built an entire house out of beer and liquor bottles. Over thirty thousand bottles were used. Many of the bottles once held Adolphus Busch beer, which later became Budweiser. Most important, Kelly's innovative use of building material paved the way for future generations of dorm rooms and frat houses decorated with beer bottle shelves and whiskey bottle walls.

The bottle house was restored and reroofed by Paramount Pictures to use as a movie setting in 1925. It was then given to the Beatty Improvement Association to be maintained as a historical site.

Rhyolite is the only ghost town with a ghostly suburb. The Goldwell Open Air Museum adjoins Rhyolite and provides a sweet touch of surrealism to the place. The museum began as a project of Belgian sculptor Albert Szukalski (1945–2000), best known for his haunting life-size shrouded figures. Besides Szukalski's ghostly rendition of the Last Supper you'll see such things as a twenty-five-foot pink woman constructed from cinder blocks, a giant mosaic tile couch, and a towering metal prospector accompanied by a penguin. The sculpture park covers eight acres and after seeing the mystical residents, it's hard to imagine Rhyolite without them.

Above: With over fifty saloons operating during Rhyolite's heyday, Tom Kelly had no shortage of building material. He constructed his house out of beer and liquor bottles. **Left:** The depot for the Las Vegas & Tonopah Railroad is one of Rhyolite's best preserved buildings. It was one of three railroads that served the town during boom times.

Above: Part of the permanent collection of the Goldwell Open Air Museum, "Icara," by Dre Peeters, revisits the Greek myth of Icarus, who flew too close to the sun. It is an apt story for this sizzling place. **Right:** The piece that launched Goldwell Open Air Museum: "The Last Supper" by Albert Szukalski. To create the ghostly figures, Szukalski wrapped live models in fabric soaked in wet plaster and posed them.

BACKCOUNTRY ROADS

KICKING ASPHALT

If you're the kind of traveler anxious to leave pavement behind and plunge into the outback, you'll love Death Valley and its hundreds of miles of dirt roads.

However, since this is *Death* Valley, plan your trip carefully. Check with rangers to find out the current condition of the road and to fill out a backcountry form. Be prepared to change tires and make sure you have the necessary tools. Carry plenty of food and water. Don't rely on technology. Your cell phone probably won't work and many GPS units are unreliable, often sending visitors down impassable and isolated roads. If in doubt, be safe and rent a Jeep.

FARABEE'S JEEP RENTALS

Richard Farabee has been in the Jeep rental business a long time. So when Death Valley visitors ask the location of the most challenging road, he levels with them.

"Moab, Utah," he says. "I know what they're after and it's a very different experience here. In Moab, they come to go 'Jeeping.' The Jeep is the activity. Here it's just safe transportation to get you to some amazing places." Farabee was asked to open

Perched on the western edge of the national park atop the Argus Mountains, Father Crowley Point dishes up a extravagant panorama. Father John J. Crowley was known as the "Desert Padre," who ministered in the area during the 1920s and '30s.

a Jeep concession by the national park service to provide that crucial safety factor as more visitors looked to slip free of the pavement. While he still operates in Moab as well as multiple locations in Colorado, he personally packed up and moved to Death Valley, another soul who fell under the spell of magnificent desolation. His Jeeps are outfitted for the remote and rugged terrain, not just with the big durable tires and sturdy suspension, but Farabee also provides an easy-to-operate SPOT Satellite GPS Messenger to be activated in case of mechanical failure or medical emergency. "This park is over three million acres," says Farabee. "When I give them this little satellite unit and explain how it works, I've just taken the worst-case scenario that was nagging at them and removed it from the equation. You shouldn't be venturing into these places without someone in the area knowing your plans and contact information." Farabee walks customers through the Jeep functions, goes over their itinerary offering driving tips, and provides them with maps as well as coolers filled with ice and water.

Farabee's Jeep Rentals is located across from the Inn at Furnace Creek. The two most popular backcountry roads in Death Valley are through Titus Canyon and to the Racetrack.

TITUS CANYON ROAD

Almost everything to love about Death Valley can be found along Titus Canyon Road—rugged mountains, colorful rock formations, a picturesque ghost town, and dramatic canyon narrows. The bonus: it gives you the best chance to spot bighorn sheep.

The road runs one-way going east to west and begins just outside the park six miles southwest of Beatty, Nevada. While the gravel road can usually be managed in a high clearance vehicle, expect rough washboard conditions and a steep climb with sharp drop-offs.

From Nevada 374, the road cuts across the Amargosa Valley and climbs into the Grapevine Mountains. It then enters upper Titanothere Canyon at White Pass, where fossil beds have been discovered among the rocks. Titanothere received its name from a rhinoceros-like creature whose 30–35 million-year-old skull was excavated here in 1933.

You'll continue climbing to Red Pass—at 5,250 feet, the highest point on the road with eye-popping views in both direc-

An intelligent bird with wide-ranging appetites, the raven is always alert to food possibilities. They won't hesitate to open unattended backpacks and help themselves to a snack.

The final leg of the Titus Canyon Road squeezes through a section of seductive, curving narrows as colorful rock walls rise hundreds of feet overhead. Not surprisingly, this section is also a popular day hike.

DESERT BIGHORN SHEEP

Most Death Valley residents are of the smaller variety—and then there are the desert bighorn sheep (*Ovis canadensis nelsoni*). These stocky, heavy-bodied sheep add a dash of majesty to the rocky cliffs of Death Valley. While both sexes develop horns, it's the heavy curling horns of the rams that are so distinctive. Their concave, elastic hooves allow bighorns to scramble up impossibly steep cliffs. They are most often seen near water sources.

Above: The Titus Canyon Road can be rough, steep, and narrow. But it might have some bad points, too.

tions. From here it's a fast drop to the town of Leadfield. Barely making a blip on the "boomtown" scene, Leadfield lasted less than a year. But if ever a town should have endured beyond the margins of its ore pockets, this is the burg—just because of its picturesque setting. Of course, you can't spend scenery. Left behind are a few shacks, debris piles, and crumbling mines.

Although many mines are open, enter at your own risk. Loose rocks, rotten timbers, unexpected vertical shafts, and shade-seeking critters should discourage you from poking around. You're a long way from help.

Beyond the ghost town, the road enters Titus Canyon. Bracketed by high limestone cliffs, their folded layers put powerful mountain building forces on display. Klare Spring is the only reliable water source in the canyon, making it an essential gathering spot for animals and humans. Bighorn sheep depend on this spring and, if you're lucky, you might spot a few.

Native Americans were also regular visitors and left behind petroglyphs scratched into the rock. Unfortunately, idiots of the modern age have damaged the ancient art. Look at—but don't touch—the petroglyphs.

Left: Ancient designs are etched into rocks surrounding Klare Spring, telling the story of the Native Americans who came before. **Right:** It's comforting to know that despite technological advancements, mysteries and magic still exist. In Death Valley, none are as profound as the moving rocks of the Racetrack.

The journey finishes with a flourish, as the walls of Titus Canyon close in around you for the final 1.5 miles. The wash seems barely wide enough to allow a vehicle to slither through in places. Cradling cliffs rise vertically beyond view overhead keeping the canyon bottom bathed in luxurious shade. This is an area best experienced on foot. Luckily, you can do just that if you're so inclined. (See Chapter 7: Hiking.) All too soon you emerge from the canyon shelter and sit blinking in the sunlight. This portion is open to two-way traffic and crosses the alluvial fan depositing you on Scotty's Castle Road. Titus Canyon Road is sometimes closed in summer because of heat and flash flood danger. Check at the Visitor Center.

THE RACETRACK

When it comes to sheer desert weirdness nothing tops the moving rocks of the Racetrack.

Nestled in a remote valley of the Cottonwood Mountains sits a dry lakebed or playa, known as the Racetrack. It is oval-shaped, about three miles long and two miles wide, and freakishly flat. The north end rises less than two inches higher than the south. Here rocks mysteriously slide across the surface cutting furrows in the sediment as they move.

Despite the speedy implication of the Racetrack moniker, getting there is anything but fast. The twenty-seven-mile gravel road begins at Ubehebe Crater and is a bouncy, teeth-rattling ride. A high clearance vehicle is strongly recommended.

The marshy wetlands of Saratoga Springs draw a wide range of resident and migrating birds such as this great blue heron.

SARATOGA SPRINGS

At the southern edge of the Ibex Hills, the lush oasis of Saratoga Springs provides crucial habitat for the Saratoga Springs pupfish (*Cyprinodon nevadensis nevadensis*) and other rare species such as the Amargosa spring snail and the Death Valley June beetle. Resident and migrating birds are regular visitors, so don't forget the binoculars. Depending on the season, keep an eye peeled for herons, egrets, ducks, Cooper's hawk, red-winged and yellow-headed blackbirds, and snowy plover among others.

Several springs feed three large pools totaling 6.6 acres in size, making Saratoga Springs the third largest marsh habitat in the park. In the 1880s, the wetlands served as an important watering hole for the twenty-mule team wagons hauling borax from the valley floor.

JOSHUA TREE

Looking like a panicked palm tree, the Joshua tree (*Yucca brevifolia*) is one of the most striking plants in Death Valley. The largest of the yuccas, the Joshua tree is an indicator species of the Mojave Desert and exists nowhere else. It was named by Mormon pioneers who saw in the tree's unique shape the image of the biblical Joshua raising his arms in prayer. The spike-leafed evergreen prefers high desert slopes, often growing in groves.

The road climbs slightly for the first few miles as it curls into the outback. Somewhere near the eight-mile mark you enter a forest of Joshua trees. The curiously twisted, spiky trees that look like they could have been plucked from Dr. Seuss's garden huddle on the low slopes along the roadway.

At just under twenty miles you arrive at Teakettle Junction, a wooden sign draped with a collection of teapots, ranging from the simple to the ornate. They clink and clank in the breeze and reflect sunlight like a prospector's gold tooth. Some of the pots are signed or adorned with stickers, slogans, and the occasional scrawled platitude.

The Racetrack comes into view a few miles before you get there, a soft beige bottomland tucked between mountains. At the north end of the playa, a jumbled thrust of quartz monzonite rises like a forgotten island. The dark outcropping is known as the Grandstand and adds a dramatic verti-

cal note to the level surface. There's parking at the edge of the lakebed, and you can walk out to the stony cluster.

Most of the moving rocks are found at the south end of the playa. Continue down the road a couple more miles to the informational sign. Park and walk out into the big empty. Here you'll find rocks that have tumbled from the nearby mountains onto the flats. Some are the size of pineapples, others as big as a motel mini-fridge. The rocks move—sometimes hundreds of feet—leaving distinct trails behind them. Some stones travel in a straight line, others in a curved arc. Some can't seem to make up their mind, leaving a zigzag pattern etched in the playa.

The mystery of joyriding boulders was solved in 2013 when scientists witnessed and recorded the phenomenon. It requires a rare combination of events starting with enough winter rain on the playa to form a shallow pond. Nighttime temperatures drop, freezing the water on top. The sun begins to thaw the ice, which breaks into large floating panels. Winds push these ice rafts against the rocks, scooting them slowly across the mud-slick surface below. How fiendishly simple! This scorched, parched land experiences ice shove, an event more common to frigid waterfronts.

Above: A remote intersection on the way to the Racetrack, Teakettle Junction has evolved into a curious little shrine. Visitors come from all over the world to leave behind an offering of a teapot. **Above right:** The cluttered outcrop of the Grandstand is the only vertical landmark amid the eerily flat expanse of the Racetrack. **Right:** Rocks have been known to slide hundreds of feet across the Racetrack playa, a devastatingly level surface.

JUST A THOUGHT

I'm no stranger to wilderness. I spend lots of time in the desert backcountry, but I never experienced a silence as profound or adamant as at the Racetrack. It wasn't just an absence of sound but a thorough debunking of sound. It became restorative. It gave me back something I didn't realize I had lost. All afternoon I lay on the hardpack, more motionless than the stones. When I sighed, the exhale of my breath sounded like the prop wash of a plane.

The surface was so smooth and precise it could have been tiled by angels. I held on tight because I was afraid of falling. I was afraid a moment like this wouldn't come around again. I closed my eyes and could hear for the first time in my life the creak of the earth as it turned on its axis.

CHAPTER 7

HIKING

WALKING TO THE SUN

Death Valley demands a vehicle. You need reliable wheels to see this park that's roughly the size of Connecticut. Yet the machine must also be abandoned. Get out and walk. Put boots on crunchy soil and propel yourself forward, or you miss the essence of Death Valley completely.

Feel the temperature on your skin. Sniff the fragrance of a desert breeze. Listen to the silence, so resonant and rich it envelops you. Hike a trail or six. Embrace your inner desert rat. These are the best day hikes of Death Valley National Park. Many, but not all, are short, easy, and ideal for families. Ranger-guided hikes are offered during the peak season of November through April.

PLAY IT SAFE

Always carry water, even in winter. A gallon per day in the summer. And here's the important thing: DRINK IT! Plenty of bodies are recovered in the desert with water still sloshing in their canteen.

Study maps and consult with park rangers before starting out.

A visitor soaks in the lavish panorama from Dante's View, gazing across the valley floor to the Panamint Mountains.

Wear appropriate footwear. Ground temperatures in the low deserts can approach two hundred degrees during summer. How do you think your plastic Crocs will hold up? Stay out of canyons if rain is predicted because of potential flash flood danger.

Dogs are not allowed on the trails. And it's way too hot to leave them in the vehicle. Think long and hard before bringing Fido. While there are many great adventures to share with your best friend, Death Valley isn't one of them.

While it's never a bad idea to carry a cell phone, don't rely on it. Cell service is rare in the park. If you are able to acquire a signal, don't be gabbing loudly, because you just *have* to tell your old college roommate where you are. Someone, quite possibly me, will come along and encourage you to respect the reverent quiet of this place with a gentle smack upside your head.

MOSAIC CANYON

So much of Death Valley intimidates. We're awestruck by the size and apprehensive of the extremes. Harsh terrain like saltpans, sand dunes, and badlands surround us. What softens the image of Death Valley are the canyons.

Those intimate gouges sliced from barren mountain ranges pull us back from the vastness and provide a refuge. We're soothed by the cozy confines of a canyon, relieved to find a place out of the blistering sun. We run our hands over water-polished stone and discover it cool to the touch. All across the park, those slender gorges harbor scenery and secrets and none more so than twisting, multicolored Mosaic Canyon.

Millions of years ago faults developed in the area. Water channeling through these faults carved Mosaic Canyon into its present size and shape. Its name refers to the distinctive jumble of minerals, or breccia, that lines the canyon walls. Breccia is created when small rock fragments are bound together in natural cement.

DEATH IN DEATH VALLEY

It's difficult to gauge how many people have perished in Death Valley since that lone casualty of the Lost 49ers, a man named Culverwell. Records were not meticulously kept and many prospectors just disappeared into the big empty.

The sheer brutality of the land poses a constant danger, even for those accustomed to it. In July 1898, Jim Dayton, caretaker of Furnace Creek Ranch, set out for supplies. He made 20 miles before the summer heat felled him. He was buried where he was found. Years later, in the twilight of his life, prospector Shorty Harris asked to be buried alongside his old friend. Their graves and monument can be found along the West Side Road on the scorched floor of Death Valley.

It's easy to underestimate the dangers of the crushing heat and unforgiving aridity. In August, 2012, ultra-runner and holder of several grueling endurance records, Michael Popov, died on a short training run. Popov gained world renown when he completed the 222-mile John Muir Trail without receiving outside assistance in just over four days. Running across the Death Valley floor, this remarkable athlete toppled over and died from heatstroke in less than 10 miles. He was thirty-four.

Despite national park status, this is still the ragged edge of the frontier. Consider this: Four German tourists, two adults and two young boys, disappeared in July 1996. Their rental van was discovered on an isolated back road with three flat tires. Massive search efforts followed, yet their remains would not be found until thirteen years later.

Don't pin your hopes on technology. Until there is an app that causes your cell phone to spray water like a fire hose, technology can't keep you alive in the wild. In some cases, our shiny gizmos can lead us deeper into danger.

In August, 2009, a woman set out on an overnight camping trip with her six-year-old son and the family dog. Without a map she followed the directions of a GPS unit, which guided them down a backcountry road into one of the most remote corners of the park. Their Jeep Cherokee became stuck and they were stranded for five days before being found by a ranger. The woman and dog survived, but tragically the boy did not.

There have been other similar incidents prompting the National Park Service to post warnings. In Death Valley, many roads shown on some GPS systems are closed or impassable. Instead of relying solely on GPS, go old-school. Carry a map, compass, and lots of water. Then pack more water. Rely on common sense. Look out your windshield. If the road seems sketchy, DON'T TAKE IT!

In the summer, stay on paved roads. And always drive with caution. The main cause of fatality in Death Valley these days is nothing more exotic than single vehicle accidents.

Right: A short hike into Mosaic Canyon leads through a beautiful slot canyon with smooth, water-polished walls.
Below: Natural Bridge, a water-carved span arching across the streambed, is just one of the many geological features on display during this canyon hike.

The trail enters the mouth of Mosaic Canyon where walls of glossy marble laced by panels of breccia wrap around you. This is a classic slot canyon of silken curves and narrow chutes. After a few hundred yards, the canyon bends to the left and opens out. This is where many people turn around. But keep going and you can hike for about two miles in the upper branches of the canyon through additional narrows. Be prepared to

do some scaling over dry falls until a large steep chute finally blocks your passage.
WHERE: *Located a quarter-mile west of Stovepipe Wells off California 190. Follow the signed dirt road for 2 miles to the trailhead.*
LENGTH: *1 to 4 miles round trip.*
DIFFICULTY: *Easy to moderate.*

NATURAL BRIDGE

Always make time to visit a natural arch, that's my motto. It's like seeing the Earth raise an eyebrow.

A natural bridge, like the one tucked away in this gently sloped canyon, is usually classified as an arch formed primarily by a current of water. Before hiking in on the sand–pebble mix of the ancient streambed, read the informational sign posted at the trailhead. It provides an excellent overview of the geologic history that you're about to see up close. Within the canyon you'll find erosion scars like cave faults and mud drips.

The fifty-foot natural bridge appears about a half mile in. Unlike the graceful sandstone arches that are signature formations of Utah, this is a rough-hewn span etched by pounding floods. The old watercourse curves around the north side of the bridge. The canyon narrows beyond the

FAST FACT
After serving as a National Park Service ranger in Death Valley, Stan Jones launched a second career as a songwriter. His first tune was a monster hit called "(Ghost) Riders in the Sky." He wrote music for John Ford movies and for Walt Disney Studios. In 1997, Jones was posthumously inducted into the Western Music Association Hall of Fame. He once saved a boy who was stranded on a 150-foot-high ridge at Natural Bridge (right).

bridge and you reach dry falls at 0.8 miles that can be climbed with care. But soon afterward a steep twenty-foot pour-off of polished stone blocks the way. As you amble back downhill to the mouth of the canyon, you're treated to nice views of the saltpan and the mighty Panamints rising beyond.

WHERE: *From California 190 travel south on Badwater Road for 13 miles to the signed turnoff for Natural Bridge. Make the left turn and follow the gravel road for 1.5 miles to the parking area.*

LENGTH: *2 miles round trip.*

DIFFICULTY: *Easy.*

GOLDEN CANYON/ GOWER GULCH

Most of Death Valley's canyon hikes are in-and-outs. You walk until something blocks the way, and then retrace your steps.

Golden Canyon gives you another option. It swings open the back door allowing access to a whole new set of wonders.

Enter Golden Canyon and follow the curving wash on a gentle uphill slant. A trail guide pamphlet is available at the trailhead. A road once penetrated Golden Canyon, which was not the soundest of planning. A four-day storm in 1976 dumped 2.3 inches of rain and the surge of water wiped out the road, leaving behind only a few scraps of asphalt. The event proved to be a blessing for hikers who get to enjoy this very personable canyon on a more intimate basis.

The Golden Canyon segment of the hike concludes at marker #10, a mile from the trailhead. You can turn around here for a nifty two-miler. If you want to continue (make sure you've got plenty of water), take the signed trail to the east that scrambles

A Death Valley resident, coyotes are opportunistic omnivores. Their favorite food is anything that fits in their mouth. **Top:** If you decide to hike beyond Golden Canyon toward Gower Gulch, you'll weave through a maze of magnificent, sculpted badlands.

up a steep gully. The sculpted vertical cliffs of Red Cathedral loom to your left, colored by the oxidation of iron. You climb across the badlands—that mudstone maze, heaped like so much melted ice cream.

The trail crests beneath the prominent jut of Manly Beacon then drops through a series of washes dotted with trail markers. You'll reach a signed junction with the left-branching trail leading to Zabriskie Point. Bear right toward Gower Gulch, a wide, rocky wash, and then just tumble downstream.

Several old mine shafts that once probed for borax and calcite have now been sealed. There is no designated trail; just stay in the main channel pointed downstream. You'll pass through a couple of easy-to-navigate chutes until finally the gulch plunges down a thirty-foot dry falls. Don't try to follow. Instead, look for the well-worn path leading north along the base of the cliffs. Follow this back to the parking lot and enjoy dandy views of the salt flats and mountains along the way.

WHERE: *On Badwater Road, 2 miles south of California 190.*

LENGTH: *2 miles round trip for Gold Canyon; 4.3 miles round trip through Gower Gulch.*

DIFFICULTY: *Easy to moderate.*

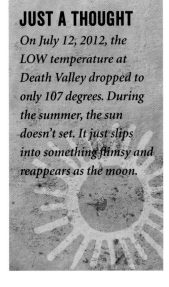

JUST A THOUGHT

On July 12, 2012, the LOW temperature at Death Valley dropped to only 107 degrees. During the summer, the sun doesn't set. It just slips into something flimsy and reappears as the moon.

Although a road cuts through Titus Canyon Narrows, the cathedral-like setting is best enjoyed on foot.

TITUS CANYON NARROWS

Hiking on a road is often Dullsville, but Titus Canyon Narrows is a big fat exception to this rule.

This soaring slot canyon marks the tail end of a popular backcountry drive. A one-way road slashes across the Grapevine Mountains and drops into Titus Canyon, culminating in the final section of narrows. Those who prefer to enter as bipeds instead of motorists can do so. The short gravel road connecting Titus Canyon to Scotty's Castle Road is two-way so you can drive to the mouth of the canyon and park.

These are sudden mountains, rising with a brutish thrust. The canyon immediately engulfs you. Although barely wide enough for a vehicle, the walls rise hundreds of feet overhead, folded and faulted and polished smooth by powerful flash floods. Cambrian age limestone adorns the walls, in places fractured into rubble and grouted together with white calcite.

The long curving passageway extends for 1.5 miles deep into the gullet of the Grapevines before finally opening outward. Turn around here or, if you've got plenty of water and stamina, continue to Klare Springs approximately 5 miles beyond the narrows. Try to get an early start. Later in the day you'll be more likely to encounter vehicles in the narrows.

WHERE: *From California 190, turn north on Scotty's Castle Road. Drive 15 miles to the Titus Canyon turnoff. Turn right onto this gravel road and drive east 2.7 miles.*

LENGTH: *3 miles round trip.*

DIFFICULTY: *Easy.*

FALL CANYON

Fall Canyon is the country cousin to nearby Titus. It cleaves the same mountains exhibiting the same geological rowdiness, but, without a road winding through, it feels more remote and isn't perfumed by exhaust fumes.

You even utilize the same trailhead. From the parking lot at Titus, a footpath runs north across low hills and gullies. After a half-mile it deposits you in the broad graveled wash that marks the entrance to Fall Canyon. Slog in on the rocky streambed. The ravine starts wide but soon high cliffs crowd forward. Canyon walls are creased with tilted fault lines, sculpted with ledges and alcoves. In places the walls pinch in, creating intimate moments of narrows.

After about 3 miles, a twenty-foot dry fall blocks the way. This is a good turn-around spot. However, some intriguing portions of the canyon lie ahead. If you wish to proceed, backtrack down the canyon for a hundred yards or so. Look for a cairned route along the south wall that will scramble up over the pour-off. Be advised this bypass requires at least moderate rock climbing ability. Nothing technical, but you should be sure of foot and hand.

Once you're beyond the slick chute, the canyon seems to inhale, with walls buckling inward forming a seductive stretch of narrows through water-polished limestone. The canyon widens out, contracts again, and then widens. You can continue through the upper section of Fall Canyon with its many different looks for an additional 3 miles or so before reaching an impassible dry fall.

WHERE: *From California 190, turn north on Scotty's Castle Road. Drive 15 miles to the Titus Canyon turnoff. Turn right onto this gravel road and drive east 2.7 miles.*

LENGTH: *6 miles round trip to visit the first dry fall.*

DIFFICULTY: *Moderate.*

DARWIN FALLS

Tucked away in a shady canyon, this year-round waterfall is at the heart of a lush oasis. It feels a world apart from the rest of the sun-chewed wilderness and that makes it all the more magical.

The hike starts in a gravel-bottomed arroyo that curves toward the mouth of the canyon. Darwin Creek supplies water to nearby Panamint Springs Resort via the pipeline you see hugging the rocky walls. As you enter the defile, clusters of willows drape the stream, and high cliffs of black rhyolite rise above. The music of water and the canopy of shade offer a sweet respite from desert heat.

The stream splashes among boulders and brush in the narrow canyon. There's no maintained trail so pick your own route, crisscrossing the water as necessary. Flooding is usually not a problem, but you'll notice woody debris wrapped around tree trunks, evidence of when the little creek turned from feisty to furious.

At about the one-mile point, the walls form a cozy cul-de-sac to frame Darwin Falls. The cascade tumbles through a narrow, frothy chute, splitting at the bottom as it slides down either side of a mossy boulder in a twenty-five-foot drop. A deep pool spreads out in front of the falls and

Below: In a land as harsh as Death Valley, the concept of an oasis takes on a whole new significance. And Darwin Falls creates a lush, soothing, and memorable oasis.

Above: Snow-capped for much of the winter, the Panamint Mountains provide a refreshing getaway when summer heat batters the valley floor.

supports a delicious population of cattails, watercress, and ferns. If you've got a picnic lunch, break it out pronto.

WHERE: *From Panamint Springs Resort, drive west on California 190 one mile to the signed turnoff for Darwin. Turn left and follow this gravel road 2.4 miles to the parking area.*

LENGTH: *2 miles round trip.*

DIFFICULTY: *Moderate.*

WILDROSE PEAK

When summer heat becomes too much to bear, the towering Panamint Mountains offer a cool refuge. The trail to Wildrose Peak begins at the charcoal kilns and climbs steadily through forests of juniper and piñon pine to reach a wind-scoured summit with wraparound views that extend well beyond the boundaries of the national park.

The trail quickly climbs onto a bench above the kilns, which look like an orderly row of stone wigwams from above. It then follows the gentle contour of the hill for the next mile as it joins an old logging road. Weathered stumps are still visible from trees cut down over a century ago to be fed into the kilns. You'll enjoy some great views

of Wildrose Canyon early on, but they're just a prelude of what's to come. A steep climb to a high saddle rewards you with stunning vistas of Badwater Basin. Over the final mile, a series of sharp switchbacks attains the 9,046-foot summit.

After traveling through fairly luxuriant woodlands (at least by Death Valley standards) it's surprising to find the summit of Wildrose swept bare with just a few grasses, shrubs and hearty cacti huddled against the wind.

WHERE: *From California 190, drive south on Emigrant Canyon Road 21 miles to the junction of Wildrose Canyon. Turn east on Wildrose Canyon Road and drive 7.1 miles to the charcoal kilns. The road is paved for the first 5 miles. The rough gravel portion can normally be managed in a sedan, but at times it may be necessary to park and walk for a bit.*

LENGTH: *8.4 miles round trip.*

DIFFICULTY: *Strenuous.*

TELESCOPE PEAK

If you wish to describe Death Valley on the cusp of summer, "snowy" probably doesn't leap to mind. Yet Telescope Peak, Death Valley's highest point at 11,049 feet, often stays buried by snow well into May.

The trail snakes up the east slope of Roger's Peak through groves of mountain mahogany, piñon pine, and juniper. Cresting a broad saddle, the trees break apart revealing sweeping views. Crossing the nearly level expanse of Arcane Meadow gives you a chance to catch your breath after the steady climb. This high meadow is often splashed with wildflowers during summer months. The final ascent chases a rocky ridgeline toward the summit. A series of lung-squeezing switchbacks slice through stands of limber pine, which grow only above nine thousand feet, mixed with ancient bristlecone pine. Telescope Peak earned its name because of the far-reaching views from the summit. The western horizon is dominated

Desert Sunflowers

Indian Paint Brush

Sand Verbena

Bigelow's Monkeyflower

Mojave Desert Star

Desert Five-spot

WILDFLOWERS

Death Valley's showiest plants make only rare appearances. Some years the desert bursts into a shimmering sea of wildflowers. If you've ever been in the desert during one of those magical years, where flowers drench the hillsides and sweep across the flats, it feels like you're inside a kaleidoscope. You never forget the experience.

Conditions need to be just right, primarily extra rain well spaced through the winter and spring. That triggers the millions of seeds lying dormant in the soil and leads to the dramatic displays from February to April. Most wildflowers are annuals, also referred to as ephemerals (short-lived).

Prominent wildflowers in Death Valley include desert gold, gravel-ghost, golden evening primrose, desert five-spot, brittlebush, and desert paintbrush.

Above: The mighty bulk of Telescope Peak shoulders above the Panamints and dominates the Death Valley skyline. The summit can be attained by a grueling yet spectacular trail.

Right: Enduring bitter cold and lashing wind, gnarled bristlecone pines cling to the high slopes of the Panamint Mountains. Some ancient specimens are nearly 5,000 years old.

by the rugged peaks of the Sierra Nevada range, including Mount Whitney, the highest point in the contiguous United States at 14,505 feet (4,421 meters). Immediately to the east lies the lowest point, Badwater Basin at 282 feet below sea level (86 meters). It's a very curious sensation to see the two extremes from one vantage point.

The hike to Telescope Peak is long and strenuous, gaining three thousand feet of elevation in seven miles. The trail is very exposed. Always carry extra layers of clothing and sun protection, no matter what the season.

WHERE: *From California 190, drive south on Emigrant Canyon Road 21 miles to the junction of Wildrose Canyon. Turn east on Wildrose Canyon Road and drive 8.6 miles to the Mahogany Flat Campground. The road is paved for the first 5 miles. The final*

1.5 miles are rough gravel but are generally okay for a high-clearance vehicle. Four-wheel drive may be necessary in winter and spring.
LENGTH: *14 miles round trip.*
DIFFICULTY: *Strenuous.*

The ceiling at Amargosa Opera House features sixteen ladies playing antique musical instruments and a sky filled with billowing clouds and dancing cherubs. It was painted by Marta Becket.

CHAPTER 8

OUTSIDE THE PARK

MEETING THE NEIGHBORS

BEATTY, NEVADA

When Shorty Harris and Ed Cross found gold in the Bullfrog Hills in 1904, several camps sprang up in the ensuing rush. Beatty, named for a local rancher, is the only surviving town of the Bullfrog Mining District, and serves as the eastern gateway to Death Valley.

Nestled in Oasis Valley, Beatty makes an ideal base camp for Death Valley exploration. The quiet desert community sits just seven miles from the national park boundary. Even closer are the ghost town of Rhyolite, the visual whimsy of Goldwell Open Air Museum, and the starting point for Titus Canyon Road.

At an elevation of 3,300 feet, Beatty provides visitors with a more temperate climate than the park. The additional trees and greenery are due to the Amargosa River, which is a river more in theory than reality since it flows mostly underground.

Several budget motels, restaurants, and saloons are scattered throughout Beatty. There's a small casino and my personal hangout, the largest candy store in Nevada. When prepping for a journey into a blazing desert, you need water, water, and more water. But there's always room for candy. And Death Valley Nut and Candy Company offers a delicious selection of everything sweet and salty you might need.

Don't leave without visiting the Beatty Museum, a treasure trove of local history. Small town museums exude such charm because they reflect the passion of that community. These aren't just dusty artifacts; they belonged to someone's grandfather and come with a story.

DEATH VALLEY JUNCTION, CALIFORNIA

Of all the strange tales surrounding Death Valley, perhaps the oddest and by far the sweetest is the story of Marta Becket and the Amargosa Opera House.

As a young woman, Becket danced at Radio City Music Hall and on Broadway. Looking to expand creatively, she developed a one-woman show and toured the country. In the spring of 1967, a fateful flat tire

Above: The town of Beatty, Nevada, perches on the eastern edge of the Death Valley National Park and includes a collection of restaurants, saloons, motels, and shops.

The beautifully resurrected Amargosa Opera House awaits another exciting performance.

prompted an unexpected stop in the lonely outpost of Death Valley Junction. While the tire was being repaired, Becket explored what remained of this old company town built by Pacific Coast Borax in the 1920s. It consisted of a U-shaped complex of Spanish Colonial style adobe buildings. Much to Becket's surprise, the largest structure turned out to be a decrepit theater. She peeked inside and saw her future.

As she later wrote, "Peering through the tiny hole, I had the distant feeling that I was looking at the other half of myself. The building seemed to be saying, 'Take me . . . do something with me . . . I offer you life.'"

Becket rented the theater, moved from New York, and made repairs. Although it was originally called Corkhill Hall, she renamed her new home Amargosa Opera House (*amargosa* is Spanish for bitter). She gave her first performance on February 10, 1968, for an audience of twelve.

With a population base of practically zero to draw from, audiences were sparse at

first. But Becket soon solved that problem. In July 1968, she began painting an entire sixteenth-century audience on the walls. King, queen, nobility, monks, nuns, American Indians, and gypsies gazed on each performance. It took four years to complete the murals and when Becket finished, she painted the ceiling.

Along the way, stories of Becket were popping up in media around the globe. Becket was no longer dancing just for murals. She entertained into her eighties, giving her final performance on February 12, 2012, but shows continue at the opera house.

Becket formed the nonprofit Amargosa Opera House Inc., which in turn bought the town of Death Valley Junction. Now listed in the National Register of Historic Places, the Amargosa Opera House & Hotel continues to welcome guests. Many rooms in the hotel include paintings by Marta Becket, and there's also a museum dedicated to this remarkable woman.

Right: Devils Hole is the smallest known habitat in the world for a single vertebrate species, the Devils Hole pupfish.

DEVILS HOLE/ASH MEADOWS NATIONAL WILDLIFE REFUGE, NEVADA

Any critter with a Death Valley address knows hard times aplenty, but none has it tougher than the fish.

The Devils Hole pupfish (*Cyprinodon diabolis*) have been totally isolated for ten to twenty thousand years. Their entire world consists of a water-filled cavern, sixty-six-feet long by fifteen-feet wide. The fish forage and spawn on a shallow rock shelf near the surface, feeding primarily on algae. They're about the size of a Goldfish snack cracker and the population fluctuates with the seasons, up to three to five hundred in the summer and one hundred or less during the winter.

In 1952, Devils Hole became part of Death Valley National Monument. The detached forty-acre unit is now surrounded by Ash Meadows National Wildlife Refuge, an area of scrubby desert and spring-fed wetlands east of Death Valley.

Ash Meadows might be the most amazing place you never heard of. Established in 1984, the refuge shelters at least twenty-six species of plants and animals found nowhere else on earth. This portion of the Mojave Desert sits atop a vast underground aquifer and Ash Meadows acts as one of the few discharge points. Over ten thousand gallons per minute flow year-round, most of which come from seven major springs.

A series of trails and wooden boardwalks weave through the ash and mesquite groves and skirt the underbrush fringing the streams. This is a great place for bird and wildlife watching.

Devils Hole is actually a fissure peering into that aquifer. The pupfish stay near the surface yet the trough plunges to an unknown depth. It's been mapped down to five hundred feet but the bottom has not been discovered.

The most inexplicable facet of Devils Hole is its ability to monitor earthquakes around the world. Eyewitness accounts, electronic monitors, and video equipment have recorded waves up to six feet following a seismic disturbance. In March 2012, a team of researchers was doing routine monitoring of Devils Hole when a magnitude 7.4 quake hit near Acapulco, some seventeen hundred miles distant, and furiously churned the waters.

Fascinating it may be, but Devils Hole lacks visual appeal. A chain link fence surrounds the "hole" and access is restricted so there's not a lot to see. But there's plenty of other eye candy at Ash Meadows so the drive is definitely worthwhile.

LONE PINE, CALIFORNIA

If any of the Death Valley communities steal your heart, Lone Pine will be the likely

FAST FACT

In 1965, three young men with scuba gear attempted an illegal exploration of Devils Hole. Two of the divers did not resurface and their bodies were never found.

DESERT TORTOISE

Slow and steady wins the race, but if you see a desert tortoise (*Gopherus agassizii*) entered in a race, don't bet the rent money. These lumbering mini-tanks spend most of their time in underground burrows, emerging after seasonal rains and in spring to munch wildflowers. They prefer the gravelly soil of creosote bush communities above three thousand feet elevation and can survive a year or more without water. The desert tortoise is the official state reptile of both California and Nevada.

culprit. The jagged wall of the Sierra Nevada Mountains form a dramatic backdrop, but it's when you cruise downtown that the charm factor really overpowers you.

This is a throw-back: an honest-to-goodness Main Street, with people ducking in and out of shops and kids skateboarding down the sidewalks. A collection of motels, restaurants, and stores are clustered in the heart of the burg with old-school neon signs adding a retro vibe. There's a pharmacy, hardware store, and market in the center of town. Not big boxes, mind you, but mom-and-pops stores.

Make time to visit the Lone Pine Film History Museum. This spacious facility opened in 2006 and is chock-full of memorabilia from nearly seven hundred movies filmed in the area. Lone Pine, with its unruly backyard that includes the Alabama Hills, a jumbled wonderland of granite boulders, has long been a Hollywood favorite almost as soon as they figured out how to make moving pictures.

The first feature film shot entirely on location at Lone Pine was *The Round-up*, a 1920 western starring Roscoe "Fatty" Arbuckle. While the wildly eroded rocks of the Alabama Hills appeared in hundreds of early westerns, they also pinch hit for northern India, the Gobi Desert, the Middle East, and Africa. Lone Pine continues to serve as a location for films and commercials, and the museum seems to have collected artifacts from all of them.

Top: The dramatic boulder fields of the Alabama Hills have been luring Hollywood filmmakers to Lone Pine since movies were first being made. **Above:** The Lone Pine Film History Museum houses a staggering array of relics, collectibles, and props from movies filmed in the area, including the elegant 1937 Plymouth Coupe driven by Humphrey Bogart in *High Sierra*.

MOVIES FILMED NEAR DEATH VALLEY

Death Valley has served as one of Hollywood's most reliable back lots. More than seven hundred movies have been filmed in and around Death Valley. Here are a few:

Death Valley (shown above)	*The Professionals*
Django Unchained	*Rocketship X-M*
Gladiator	*Spartacus*
The Greatest Story Ever Told	*Star Wars*
Gunga Din	*Three Godfathers*
Iron Man	*Tremors*
One-eyed Jacks	*Zabriskie Point*

Voted one of the worst fifty movies of all time, Michelangelo Antonioni's 1970 counterculture cult film *Zabriskie Point* eventually won acclaim for the "stark beauty of its cinematography" for the Death Valley scenes.

SHOSHONE, CALIFORNIA

Situated amid the mesquite *bosques* (riverside thickets) of the Amargosa River, Shoshone offers some riparian respite from the surrounding desert. Originally founded as a rail stop of the Tonopah and Tidewater Line in 1909, the little town retains its historic character while offering services for people entering Death Valley from the south.

Besides a general store and gas station, there's a motel, eatery, and another surprising museum. This one displays an entire mammoth skeleton unearthed nearby. The Crowbar Café & Saloon was built in the 1930s, a classic diner from that era with a long counter flanked by tables and dishing up scratch-made cuisine. The Shoshone Inn is a cozy mid-century motor court. Guests also enjoy a warm springs swimming pool.

If you've got extra time, a network of easy trails explore the Shoshone Wetland Preserve. This thousand-acre private nature sanctuary is a birding hotspot.

A few miles southeast of Shoshone you'll find a couple of unexpected jewels. First, Tecopa, a wisp of a community that harbors a network of natural hot springs. The campground features showers and men's and women's enclosed hot mineral pools where clothing is forbidden. Strip, shower, and then join your new best friends in the water, au naturel. If you're the shy type, a couple of small motels in town offer private pools. The waters of Tecopa are famous for their restorative powers.

Even more surprising is beautiful China Ranch Date Farm. Hidden away among scorched badlands, this working family farm is the very definition of an oasis. Follow the road into a seemingly barren wasteland and, just when you start thinking this was someone's idea of a joke, you drop through a narrow cut in the hills, past arches and scars of gypsum mines. Suddenly you reach the bottom of the canyon where a verdant spread awaits.

The first date palms were planted from mail-order seeds. Today, Brian Brown continues the family tradition, harvesting twelve hundred trees. All dates are grown without the use of herbicides or pesticides and he specializes in Old World varieties.

A gift shop and bakery sell gift boxes and fresh made goodies like date nut bread, muffins, cookies, and the best date shake I ever gulped. There are self-guided nature walks and picnic tables on the grounds. When you're sitting in the shade sipping a date shake listening to the splash of Willow Creek, don't forget to remind yourself that you're in the middle of the Mojave Desert. Weird, huh?

Mats of sand verbena are just some of the wildflowers that appear in spring following winter rains.

CHAPTER 9

EAT, SLEEP, SHOP & LEARN

NATIONAL PARK

The Furnace Creek Visitor Center is the primary visitor information source for Death Valley. It was originally built in 1959 and underwent an extensive, eco-friendly makeover in 2012. Detailed interpretive displays will answer your geology, climate, and wildlife questions. Plus, this is where you'll get all the latest road conditions, as well as backcountry/hiking information and permits. A lavishly photographed park film is shown several times daily and well worth viewing.

Also at the visitor center, the Death Valley Natural History Association (DVNHA) maintains a comprehensive gift shop and bookstore. DVNHA is a non-profit association dedicated to the preservation and interpretation of the Death Valley region and is partnered with the National Park Service. They contribute all profits to benefit education and research in Death Valley National Park and Ash Meadows National Wildlife Refuge.

National park facilities can also be found at Stovepipe Wells Ranger Station and Scotty's Castle Museum.

The park service maintains nine campgrounds that vary in size, amenities, and elevation. Those on the valley floor will be too hot in summer. Only the Furnace Creek campground takes reservations and the rest operate on a first-come, first-served basis.

Backcountry camping is available throughout the park with some restrictions. Free permits for backcountry camping may be obtained at the visitor center or any ranger station.

LODGING

The first tourists to Death Valley had to kill and eat their oxen to survive. I'm happy to report that services have improved considerably since then.

FURNACE CREEK

If Death Valley has a downtown, it is Furnace Creek, a busy little hub surrounding a permanent water source. A swath of commerce has sprung up in the shade of the palm trees, known as the Furnace Creek Resort. The property hosts two hotels— the historic four-diamond Inn at Furnace Creek and the more family oriented Ranch at Furnace Creek.

Luxury and pampering are not words normally associated with this inhospitable land, but you'll find plenty of both at the elegant Inn at Furnace Creek. Opened in 1927 by the Pacific Coast Borax Company, the resort features sixty-six beautiful rooms, a fine restaurant, and amenities such as a natural spring-fed swimming pool, lush

Fine dining and spectacular views are part of the luxurious charm of Furnace Creek Inn.

palm gardens, golf, tennis, massages, horseback rides, and more.

The Ranch at Furnace Creek has been welcoming guests since 1933. Amid the complex of 224 cabins and motel rooms, you'll find three restaurants, a saloon, a general store, and the Borax Museum. Guests will also enjoy a swimming pool fed by natural spring flow, tennis and bocce courts, horse-drawn carriages, horseback rides, and a chance to tee off on the world's lowest golf course, at 214 feet below sea level. The 18-hole par 70 course was redesigned by noted golf course architect Perry Dye.

The Ranch at Furnace Creek is open year round. Both the Inn and the Ranch are operated by Xanterra Parks & Resorts, the nation's largest park management company.

STOVEPIPE WELLS VILLAGE

Herman "Bob" Eichbaum was one of the first to see the tourism potential of Death Valley. He decided to build a spectacular resort near Hell's Gate. The fact that no road existed didn't dissuade him. In 1925, Eichbaum began carving out a toll road to encourage California tourists to visit.

Eichbaum's plans turned out to be bigger than his wallet. His road fizzled twelve miles shy of his destination. He was forced to build a scaled-down version of

his hotel, now just a handful of bungalows. Bungalette opened November 1, 1926. The name was later changed to Stovepipe Wells Hotel. And thanks to the attractive dunes, the location didn't turn out to be so bad.

In addition to eighty-three motel rooms of varying sizes, Stovepipe Wells Village also includes gas pumps, a gift shop, and a general store. There's also Badwater Saloon and the aptly named Toll Road Restaurant, a nice tribute to a visionary's dream.

PANAMINT SPRINGS

Panamint Springs Resort is a family-owned operation, the only one in the National Park. Sitting at the base of the Argus Range on the western edge of Panamint Valley, this rustic resort includes a fifteen-unit motel, gas station convenience store, campground, and a dandy restaurant with a great patio.

The eatery features an extensive collection of over 170 different beers. Sitting on the patio with the sprawl of Panamint Valley below and a twilight bruising the skyline, it is a temptation to stay long enough to try each and every one.

Panamint Springs Resort also serves as an excellent starting point if you're looking to explore some of the more remote areas of the park such as Saline Valley and Hunter Mountain.

Made famous by the Warner Bros. cartoon, the roadrunner uses its surprising speed to catch and eat just about anything that walks, crawls, or flies, including rattlesnakes.

Above: Only the toughest athletes compete in the Badwater Ultramarathon, which is the equivalent of running five back-to-back marathons in the unforgiving Death Valley heat.

EVENTS

BADWATER ULTRAMARATHON

The natural extremes of Death Valley inspired humans to concoct their own—like staging a race from the lowest point in the contiguous United States to the highest. And since this is the hottest place in the world, why not hold it in the middle of July? Welcome to the Badwater Ultramarathon, hailed as "the world's toughest footrace."

Starting at Badwater, 282 feet below sea level, runners brave the blistering heat to run across Death Valley and climb three mountain ranges ending on Mt. Whitney, a distance of 135 miles. If they complete the course within forty-eight hours they're awarded—wait for it—a belt buckle. Among elite ultra-runners, buckling at Badwater is akin to winning the Super Bowl, an Academy Award, and getting a puppy on Christmas morning, all rolled into one. The Badwater Ultramarathon is an annual race managed by AdventureCORPS°, an athlete-run firm promoting extreme sports events and lifestyle.

DEATH VALLEY '49ERS ENCAMPMENT

The Death Valley '49ers are an all-volunteer, nonprofit organization that seeks to expand awareness of Death Valley. The group sponsors Death Valley's most popular event: the Annual Encampment. The five-day shindig held in November is meant to celebrate the courageous spirit of the 1849 pioneers that crossed Death Valley. Each year the Encampment draws a crowd of several thousand.

Festivities include a wagon train, horse parades, pioneer costume contest, art show, cowboy poetry, old-time music, and plenty more. The first Encampment was held during California's centennial in 1949 and proved to be such a huge success that it became an annual tradition. Proceeds from the Encampment funds a scholarship program for Death Valley area students.

ACKNOWLEDGMENTS

The author wishes to acknowledge the invaluable assistance of several people. The National Park Service and the perpetually cheerful and courteous rangers of Death Valley, Phyllis Nefsky, Phil Dickinson and the staff of Xanterra Parks and Resort for their hospitality, the Death Valley National History Association for their tireless work, the Death Valley '49ers for preserving the heritage of this harsh land, and Chris Kostman and AdventureCORPS for giving the crazies a place to run. Thanks to the terrific Rio Nuevo team. And a special thanks to Jill Cassidy, the most gracious and accommodating of editors who rearranges entire schedules for my little side projects; Peter Aleshire, whose early support and encouragement meant more than he will ever know; and most importantly my wife, Michele, whose faith, patience, and love knows no bounds.

ABOUT THE AUTHOR

Roger Naylor is a Southwestern travel writer and humorist. His work has appeared in *Arizona Republic, USA Today, Go Escape, Arizona Highways, Western Art & Architecture,* and *Route 66 Magazine.* He is a senior writer for The Bob and Tom Show, a nationally syndicated radio program airing in over 150 markets. His first book, *Arizona Kicks on Route 66* was released in 2012. For more information, visit www.rogernaylor.com.

INFORMATION AND RESOURCES

AdventureCORPS Badwater
Ultramarathon
www.badwater.com

Amargosa Opera House & Hotel
760-852-4441
www.amargosaoperahouse.com

Ash Meadows National Wildlife Refuge
775-372-5435
www.fws.gov/desertcomplex/ashmeadows

Beatty Museum
775-553-2303
www.beattymuseum.org

Beatty Chamber of Commerce
775-553-2424
www.beattynevada.org

China Ranch Date Farm
760-852-4415
www.chinaranch.com

Death Valley '49ers
www.deathvalley49ers.org

Death Valley National Park
PO Box 579
Death Valley, CA 92328
760-786-3200
www.nps.gov/deva/index.htm

Death Valley Natural History Association
PO Box 188
Death Valley, CA 92328
www.dvnha.com

Death Valley Nut and Candy Company
775-553-2100

Farabee's Jeep Rentals
760-786-9872
www.deathvalleyjeeprental.com

Furnace Creek Campground
877-444-6777

Furnace Creek Resort
760-786-2345
www.furnacecreekresort.com

Goldwell Open Air Museum
702-870-9946
www.goldwellmuseum.org

Lone Pine Chamber of Commerce
760-876-4444
www.lonepinechamber.org

Museum of Lone Pine Film History
760-876-9909
www.lonepinefilmhistorymuseum.org

Panamint Springs Resort
775-482-7680
www.panamintsprings.com

Scotty's Castle
760-786-2392

Shoshone Village
760-852-4250
www.shoshonevillage.com

Stovepipe Wells Village
760-786-2387
www.escapetodeathvalley.com

Tecopa Hot Springs Campground
760-852-4481
www.clm-services.com

PHOTO CREDITS
All photos are copyrighed by the photographers